BEFORE YOU
SAVE THE DATE

21 QUESTIONS
to help you marry with confidence

Before You Save the Date may well be the second most important book you ever read. That's not hyperbole.

If you're contemplating a less-than-wise marital relationship, and God uses the wisdom contained in *Before You Save the Date* to get you to re-evaluate your decision, no book, other than the Bible, will have a greater impact on your life. If you're not dating anyone at the moment, and *Before You Save the Date* helps guide you to someone who would make a wonderful marriage partner, you'll be blessed for the rest of your life. That's how important the information contained in this book really is.

Gary Thomas
Author of Sacred Marriage

. . . .

Beware! Marrying without asking the right questions can lead someone down the aisle with the wrong person. Be careful of saving the date until you have read *Before You Save the Date*, an immensely practicable, user-friendly guide for anyone considering marriage—the second most important decision in life.

Jess Bousa
Author of The Discipleship Dare *and Associate Pastor, Grace Assembly of God, Bel Air, MD*

. . . .

After engagement we often get so into the "wedding mode" we forget to prepare for the marriage. *Before You Save the Date* will help couples take an honest look at their relationship and ask the tough questions that will become the foundation of a Godly and lasting marriage.

Kirsten V. Watson
Co-Founder of Watson One More Foundation, Boston, MA

. . . .

Through insight and experience, Dr. Friesen posits the hard questions we should ask ourselves before making the second most important decision in life. With honest examination, our answers to these questions will either affirm the relationship or protect us from settling for anything less than God's best. Besides serving as a helpful tool, these questions will be a springboard for intimate discussions with the person we're planning to spend our lives with . . . and prepare us for our journey ahead together.

Derek B. Johnson
Executive Director, CURE Children's Hospital of Uganda

. . . .

Before You Save the Date has been one of the most valuable resources that we have used in our pre-marriage program. It has been the foundation for some very meaningful dialogue between our couples around subjects that until now they may have avoided or not thought to explore.

Ron Perry
Pastor of Marriage, Church of the Saviour, Wayne, PA

What participants in pre-marital classes are saying about *Before You Save the Date*

My boyfriend and I had already spent countless hours answering questions about each other in an effort to get to know each other better quickly. We printed out "questions to ask before marriage" from the Internet and I purchased a book with a lot of questions. We were surprised that your list contained a lot of questions we had not encountered yet. The questions definitely brought to light some things we hadn't discussed yet and helped us engage in meaningful discussions. It was great to have challenging questions to talk through.

—*Karen*

Before You Save the Date allowed one of us to bring up a difficult topic that was never broached before. It brought clarity to certain topics . . . we want to work on the issues that came up and commit to change even before entering into marriage.

—*Tara*

Made us think a bit more seriously about certain areas of our relationship and raised an issue or two that we realize that we will need to work on, instead of being a surprise later.

—*Sue*

In general, this whole process is bringing us together and helping us to want to know each other more deeply. We understand our future commitment for life, and if anything, we are just getting more excited.

—*Tom and Kerryn*

Before You Save the Date was thought provoking and allowed for great times of discussion with my partner. The "Making it Personal" section was particularly appreciated.

—*Janessa*

We now have a better understanding of what we will have to work extra hard on and what topics will be issues for us. We were also able to see things we appreciate about our partner and things they are doing well.

—*Caroline*

Before You Save the Date taught us that it is important to address and unpack issues as they arise. This exercise brought to light questions that we may have touched on in the past but this gave us the forum to discuss them more openly. It is our hope that we can continue to build on this experience.

—*Keith and Angie*

BEFORE YOU
SAVE THE DATE

21 QUESTIONS
to help you marry with confidence

DR. PAUL FRIESEN

Home Improvement Ministries
Bedford, Massachusetts

BEFORE YOU SAVE THE DATE

ISBN: 978-0-9789931-5-3

Published by HOME IMPROVEMENT MINISTRIES.
For information on other H.I.M. resources, please contact:
HOME IMPROVEMENT MINISTRIES, 209 Burlington Road, Bedford, MA 01730.
E-mail inquiries: info@HIMweb.org
Website: www.HIMweb.org

Unless otherwise noted, all scripture quotations are from the HOLY BIBLE: NEW INTERNATIONAL VERSION. Copyright © 1973, 1978, 1984 by the International Bible Society.

Printed in the United States of America.   4/10TPS2000

To the hundreds of couples that we have been privileged to counsel and lead through Engagement Matters.
May you experience all that God designed marriage to be.

Acknowledgments

Special thanks to Nate and Jennie King, Ryan and Kelly Plosker, Brian and Heather Dietz, Doug and Julie Macrae, Dan and Wendy Taylor, and Jess and Elizabeth Bousa for their input on the manuscript.

Secondly, I want to thank the Home Improvement Ministries board, who have made it possible for Virginia and me to do the things we love doing.

Thirdly, special thanks to Barbara and Guy Steele, who have done all the formatting, design, and editing of this book. Without them, my rocks would never be turned into gems.

Fourthly, thanks to Doug and Julie Macrae for providing a place for us to write and be refreshed in the process.

Fifthly, I am deeply appreciative of our daughters Julie, Lisa, and Kari and Kari's husband Gabe for their input on this project and the passion they have given me to help couples think more clearly about relationships.

Sixthly, even though my name is on the cover of this book, it truly is an effort by both Virginia and me. After 33 years of marriage, there are few thoughts we haven't processed together. Thanks, Virginia, for partnering in life and ministry. God gave me the perfect "excellent wife" in you and so much of who I am is because of your love for me.

Lastly, without the work of the Holy Spirit, this book is just a partial destruction of a tree. Thank you, Father, for giving me life and for giving me a purpose in living. Any benefit this book may be is due to your grace and love. May you receive any glory given.

Contents

.

Foreword

Before You Save the Date may well be the second most important book you ever read.

That's not hyperbole.

If you're contemplating a less-than-wise marital relationship, and God uses the wisdom contained in *Before You Save the Date* to get you to re-evaluate your decision, no book, other than the Bible, will have a greater impact on your life. If you're not dating anyone at the moment, and *Before You Save the Date* helps guide you to someone who would make a wonderful marriage partner, you'll be blessed for the rest of your life. That's how important the information contained in this book really is.

It's difficult to overstate the importance of making a wise marital choice. Second only to your decision to follow God, who you marry will color every aspect of your life for the rest of your life—how you spend your weekends, the social atmosphere in your home, the amount of spiritual support you have (or don't have) in your life, the parenting and role modeling your future kids will grow up with, how you'll spend your old age, what you do on vacations, holidays, evenings, and more.

Such a monumental decision demands monumental attention, vigilance, and deliberation. Sadly, this decision is most commonly made on the basis of sexual chemistry—an immediate attraction that is powerful to the point of being overwhelming, but that also always fades sooner rather than later. The Friesens get it right when they suggest that while sexual chemistry is important, it should only be about fourth or fifth on your list of what really matters. Its presence does not, on its own, signify a wise choice. Its absence is a cause for concern, but not the primary concern.

There's science to back up this wisdom. Western forms of "love style" marriages typically start out white hot and quickly cool; Eastern arranged marriages mostly start out somewhat cool and gradually heat up. Longitudinal studies have shown that the two forms of marital affection "meet up" at about year five, as the Westernized marriage is headed down and the Eastern marriage is headed up. A decade into the marriage, the arranged marriage is typically much more intimate and satisfying to both partners than the western ones.

By the way, eastern "love marriages" share the same trajectory as western ones, leading most to conclude that it's the arranging, not the culture, that influences this dynamic.

Am I suggesting we go back to arranged marriages in the west? Not necessarily (though I do think you ignore your parents' opinion at your peril)—but what we can learn from this is the need to use the same basis that arranged marriages focus on to evaluate "love marriages." In other words, "love marriages" should be tested by the same types of questions and considerations that parents who are arranging marriages for their children use in their choices. That's exactly what *Before You Save the Date* will help you to do: look at your marriage from an objective basis, and make your choice based on things that truly matter.

Again, I can't stress how much of your future happiness depends on this. If you make one bad financial investment, you can always start over, but biblical marriage is a one-shot deal. Many Christians believe there are a couple biblically "accepted" causes for divorce, but these are limited and severe. In the vast majority of cases, should you be disappointed in your choice, your obligation as a believer will be to work it out instead of walking out. It's worth the time, effort, and even the heartache of a breakup to make sure you're making a wise decision before you enter into marriage.

But more than being merely a tool to evaluate your relationship, *Before You Save the Date* can also help you build a new level of intimacy as you contemplate each question together. It will encourage you to talk about things that really matter, and it will help you gain a greater understanding of your current romantic attraction.

Please read this book prayerfully, with your heart and eyes wide open. If any red flags appear, don't even think about ignoring them, or downplaying their importance. Immediately focus on the potentially troublesome issue, talk it over with a parent, pastor, or counselor, and make sure it doesn't signal a serious problem that will undercut the intimacy of your future home. Far better to postpone or cancel an ill-advised marriage, than to go forward "hoping" the red flag is just a red herring.

If you can go through this book in an honest and prayerful fashion, recognizing weaknesses and tendencies but no real serious threats, then your marriage day will be all the more joyful. You can truly celebrate the beginning of a lifelong union with a much higher degree of confidence, because you will know that it is based on the solid foundation of wisdom instead of the eroding sinkhole of feelings.

Gary Thomas
Bellingham, Washington
author of *Sacred Marriage*

How to Use This Tool

If you are a couple, I would encourage you each to have your own copy of this book so that you can individually read each question one at a time and jot down your thoughts. Set aside some regular time to go over your observations with each other. The "Make It Personal" questions listed at the end of each chapter are there to help you individually to further process the issues presented. The "Make It Plural" section gives you space to jot down the issues that your reading of the chapter and the "Make It Personal" questions have raised; then take some time to process these together. Remember to be honest in your discussions. Simply saying what the other will want to hear may lead to an easier discussion in the moment, but does not lead to an honest relationship in the future.

I suggest that you attempt to work through the 21 Questions in approximately one month's time. Whether you are engaged, pre-engaged, or just dating, these questions could be used to bring you closer together and clarify your relationship.

If you are an individual who is not in a relationship, I encourage you to read through this book and use the 21 Questions as a guide as you consider relationships you may be entering.

If you are a parent, these questions will help you to consider the characteristics of the future spouse you are praying for on behalf of your child. In addition, this book would be an excellent gift for each of your single children.

If you are a pastor, these questions can serve as conversation starters to aid you in your pre-marital counseling curriculum.

I don't care who you are
Where you're from
What you did
As long as you love me

Thus went the lyrics of a once popular tune. As ludicrous as the chorus sounds, many couples today adhere to similar advice in making one of the most important decisions of their lives—whom to marry.

Before You Save the Date is designed to help couples be a bit more objective as they evaluate their mutual "fit" for marriage.

My wife Virginia and I believe marriage is terrific. Marriage is one of God's greatest ideas ever. Someone once said that being married to the right person is the closest thing to heaven on earth and being married to the wrong person is the closest thing to hell on earth—and we agree.

Virginia and I have counseled far too many couples, married less than three years, who are miserable in their marriages. Many of them simply want out. Often, when questioned about their issues and if there were any indicators of problems before their marriage, a couple will answer, "Yes, but we overlooked the problems because we were in love" or, "I thought he (or she) would change after marriage."

We have had more than one couple tell us they didn't want to meet with us prior to getting married because they were afraid we would raise questions that might postpone or even raise doubts about their suitability for marriage. Our goal, however, is not to break couples up, but to help individuals see themselves and their significant others more clearly as they prepare for the possibility of marriage.

The 21 questions that follow are divided into four sections.

- CONVICTIONS: Many of these questions have to do with values, faith, and convictions, especially regarding the role of scripture.

- CHARACTER: These questions address how convictions are lived out in day-to-day life—in other words, who you are when no one is looking.

- COMPATIBILITY: These questions are related to lifestyle issues, activities you enjoy, and your backgrounds.

- CHEMISTRY: These questions concern your attraction to each other—your "chemistry"—and the importance of it prior to and in marriage.

This is not a test. You don't pass or fail. The desire is for confirmation and clarity about this most important relationship. Enjoy the process.

Questions on
*C*onvictions

1 / *The Authenticity Question*

Who was this person before you met one another?

Many individuals experience dramatic changes when they meet their "true love," only to return to their previous patterns after marriage. Does she suddenly like sports? Has he lost a significant amount of weight since you met? Did he finally land his first job as an adult? Does everyone say you must be good for her, because she sure is nicer now than before she met you? Yes, God is able to change us, but often what you *didn't* see is what you are actually getting—not what you are seeing while dating.

Many pre-marital books talk about expectations in marriage. They pose such questions as, "Given a free Saturday, what would you choose to do?" Typical answer: "Anything, as long as it is with you, dear." That may be the answer every fiancé is longing to hear, but it has little relevance to how those Saturdays will actually be spent after you marry. The better question is, "Before you began seeing one another, how did you each spend your Saturdays?" Naturally, single people try to be compatible with those with whom they are pursuing a relationship. Ultimately, however, this effort to be compatible will break down if it goes against the grain of how one normally lives life.

A number of years ago, a woman in Boston met a Red Sox player at a party. The two hit it off and their conversation soon turned to sports. The Red Sox player asked the young woman if she liked baseball. He was hoping she would say "yes," of course, which was the answer the young lady offered. Thrilled, the Red Sox player said the team was in town the following weekend and would she like a ticket to the game? She gladly accepted the ticket and suggested they get together at half time. Unfortunately, there is no "half time" in baseball.

In her effort to be "compatible" with her prospect, this woman was not true to her history. I am not suggesting people are incapable of change when they love someone, but examining the historical patterns of your new love interest is often most telling.

My wife Virginia and I were talking recently about the patterns we saw in each other 30 years ago. In fact, I appeared to have changed before we were married. I lost 30 pounds before the wedding so I would "look good" for Virginia. Thirty years later, I continue to find those 30 pounds over and over again.

Hear some of the many stories we've listened to:

A man is presently out of work, but he says after he gets married he will land a good job. His girlfriend lends him money to repair his car, and pays when they dine out until he gets back on his feet. He may not have a job, but at least he always has time for her, unlike her workaholic dad. The wedding is beautiful; she pays for it, since he was a bit short on cash. Fast-forward five years. He kisses her good-bye as she goes to work. He assures her he will get out of bed soon and look for a job today. She wants to start a family, but someone has to make a living, and right now that someone is her.

A sedentary young woman falls in love with an outdoorsman. Before long she has lost weight, purchased a bicycle, and becomes a new woman. Fast-forward ten years and two children: she has not ridden the bike in years, the weight has returned, and her husband feels deceived.

She kisses him good-bye as she heads off to church with the kids. She wishes he would go to church with them. He started going to church with her before they were married and promised to continue. She did notice that he never seemed to attend church when she was out of town, but he said it was just because he was shy and didn't know anyone.

He noticed her house was always messy, but she told him that once they were beyond the stress of the wedding, she would keep the house clean again.

Is it possible to shout on the printed page? **Wake up and smell the coffee!** Virginia and I have talked to many couples in significant marital distress or who are presently divorced, who when asked if before their marriage they could foresee the issues that eventually led to their distress or divorce, each person answered yes. In each case, they said they thought the issue would change or ultimately not be that important. It was!

Love for your fiancé can drive you to appear compatible. For most people, however, the pressure of pretending to be someone other than one's natural self eventually takes its toll.

An 8th-grade girl came home, announced to her parents that she was in love with Joey, and wanted to know if she could "date" him, which meant hanging around with him and calling him her boyfriend. The parents told their daughter that she was too young to "date" anyone, but she could "hang out" with Joey as long as they were either at school or at her home with her parents. To add to the drama, Joey was the "bad boy" at school. People were shocked that such a nice, smart, well-mannered girl would be hanging around with a "bad boy" like Joey. Soon the teachers were all amazed as Joey started coming to school on time, actually bringing his books to class and doing the homework. Something had come over Joey—he was a changed boy, so it seemed, until about two weeks into the "relationship." Joey couldn't take it any more and went back to being the "bad boy." He had tried to be compatible with his girlfriend and her family's values, but he couldn't stand the pressure and reverted back to who he really was.

I do believe in God being able to change a person, but I am concerned when decisions that will affect a lifetime are made after observing changes for only a short period of time.

Making It Personal

- Talk to her friends and listen to what they have to say about the patterns in her single life.

- Take note of changes your beloved is making "for you."

- Do your family and friends think you have "changed"?

- Does the other's car, room, or clothes indicate anything about a tendency toward neatness or messiness?

- Does your fiancé have a reputation for being overly fussy about details?

- What does his "history" reveal about his work ethic?

- Take a good look backwards; your fiancé will likely return to previous patterns before too long.

Making It Plural

Jot down notes and discuss the areas this question confirmed for you or the issues that were raised in your mind which merit further discussion.

Circle the number that best represents how you feel about your relationship in light of The Authenticity Question.

10	9	8	7	6	5	4	3	2	1

Extremely confident   ⟵   ⟶   Extremely hesitant

2 / The Faith Question

Are you at a compatible level of faith?

If you are a Christian, how about your significant other? Ideally, you should desire to marry not just another Christian, but a vital Christian who will challenge you and help you to grow in your faith. Does your special friend believe in God's Word and seek to obey it in its entirety?

When the couple met one summer, the young woman made it clear to the handsome man—who was obviously interested in her—that she was a Christian and a virgin and both were very important to her. In fact, she said she intended to be a virgin going into her wedding night. He said that he, too, was a Christian, went to church, and would respect her moral position. Before long, however, their physical involvement increased and the woman became pregnant. The "right" thing to do, she thought, was to marry him, since she was pregnant and he said he was a Christian. They soon married and he began to engage in activities that were not consistent with a person of faith. He started giving excuses for not going to church and had other "pressing" matters that kept him from participating in activities that would deepen his faith. Before long, the young woman was very disillusioned. The man she had covenanted to live with for the rest of her life clearly did not share her relationship with the Lord. The closer she grew to the Lord, the more distant her husband became to her.

There is little mystery in why the Apostle Paul tells us not to be unequally yoked with unbelievers (2 Corinthians 6:14). At the very core of who we are is our faith position. A couple that does not grapple with faith compatibility before marriage is in for some rude awakenings. Regular attendance at church should be a vital expression of a Christian's faith. This is likely the reason the writer of Hebrews wrote not to neglect regular meetings with other believers (Hebrews 10:25). The mate who does not share this vital faith will not likely want to "squander" every Sunday sitting in church, when you could be out as a couple or family enjoying nature. Scripture speaks of giving 10% of your gross income to the work of the Lord as an act of obedience (Matthew 23:23). The partner without faith thinks his spouse must be crazy to voluntarily give $8,000 a year of their $80,000 income to the church. Why, that money could buy the boat they've always hoped for—or the new car they've always wanted. "It's fine to toss a bill in here and there, but let's not go overboard!" Your faith and devotion to the Lord will affect what movies you watch, what activities you engage in, what friends you choose, and more.

If faith is vital to you but not to your partner, some very rough times likely lie ahead, because your view of absolutes will tend to differ. This may seem insignificant now, but often it becomes much more pronounced when children arrive and decisions must be made as to their faith instruction or lack thereof.

Authors Jack and Cynthia Heald state the importance of a vital relationship with the Lord when they say that a man walking closely with his Lord will be a man rightly related to his wife, and a woman walking closely with her Lord will be a woman rightly related to her husband (*Walking Together*).

We cannot overstate the value of the two of you sharing the same moral beliefs. Thus far, I have focused on relationships where one person is a person of faith and one is not. This principle also applies where the level of conviction or passion regarding faith differs. For the couple where one partner is much more serious about faith, many of the same issues arise. In fact, their conflicts may be more frustrating. If a couple enters marriage knowing one does not have a faith position, there are no expectations of a shared faith. For the couple where both profess faith, but for one it is a much deeper conviction, trouble may often be delayed, but is almost certain to come. The stronger Christian is tempted to believe that the less committed Christian will mature. Unfortunately, it is a whole lot easier to pull someone down than to pull someone up. It is essential to marry someone who is at a similar position in his or her faith walk and passions.

It is important to explore your positions of faith, theology, and doctrine as well. Just yesterday, I heard a young man, who is a very strong Christian, inform a young woman, who is equally strong in her faith, that they would not be pursuing a relationship because she was not "pentecostal" enough for him. This is a case where both individuals have a vital faith, but it is expressed in ways that are very different and this difference would likely bring tension in the marriage.

Virginia and I recently met with a married couple, both Christians, but committed to faith traditions that had them attending different churches on Sundays. Their "I'll do my thing, you do yours" was now becoming more complicated as their children were growing and they each felt strongly the children should be raised in their particular faith tradition. Do you feel very strongly about doctrinal issues such as baptism, women as elders in the church, or expressions of gifts of the Holy Spirit? Better to explore these before the altar than have tension after the altar.

Making It Personal

- What were your significant other's patterns in the area of faith before you met?

- What role does the church have in the other's life when you are not together?

- What personal habits of spiritual development do you observe?

- Does your intended show any interest in spiritual development when you are not involved?

- What role does God seem to play in everyday decisions?

- When it comes to encouraging each other to grow in faith, what role does your partner play?

- Is your personal relationship with the Lord more vital because of your partner's influence?

- Do you share a similar commitment regarding church attendance?

- Are your views about media and lifestyle issues similar?

Making It Plural

Jot down notes and discuss the areas this question confirmed for you or the issues that were raised in your mind which merit further discussion.

Circle the number that best represents how you feel about your relationship in light of The Faith Question.

| 10 | 9 | 8 | 7 | 6 | 5 | 4 | 3 | 2 | 1 |

Extremely confident   ←———————→   Extremely hesitant

3 / The Word-of-God Question

Is the other's life truly governed by God's Word?

Is your beloved's life truly governed by God's Word? In times of stress and difficulty in marriage, you want to have chosen a spouse who is obedient to God's Word—even during difficult times. Does the other see obedience to God's Word as an option rather than a mandate? Choose a spouse who is more interested in honoring God and obeying His Word than in pursuing one's immediate desires.

A 40-year-old woman's husband had left her a number of years ago. She had two teenage children whom she had raised with very clear boundaries in regards to dating a person with whom one did not share a common faith. She also taught them very clear boundaries regarding physical involvement prior to marriage. Her children were disillusioned when their mother began to date a non-Christian. One evening, they walked in on their mom and her friend, finding them more involved physically than they had ever been taught was right. The mom, defending her actions said, "What do they think I am, a 16-year-old?"

But God's Word on sexual purity has no age limit nor qualifiers—even for those who have been married before.

A woman who had dated non-Christian guys for many years made the decision to date only Christians. She was a bit shocked and very disappointed to discover little difference between the

*behavior of the Christian men and those who had no rela-
tionship with Christ. These "Godly" men were able to some-
how shelve their Biblical convictions when it came to physical
involvement in dating.*

The examples are endless, but the issue is the same. Is God's
Word the final answer for all question and decisions, or are issues
to be decided on more of a case-by-case basis?

I recently gave a talk on Psalm 119 in which I discussed the
concept of true happiness being promised to those who obeyed
God's Word fully. I mentioned how difficult it is to fully obey
God's Word and how much easier it would be if we could cut
out the more difficult or objectionable sections. Consider, for
example, Malachi 3:6–10, where we are told to tithe our income;
or Philippians 4:8, where we are told to think only about things
that are pure, right, noble, or admirable; or Ephesians 5:3, where
we are told not to have even a hint of sexual immorality among
us. Much to the horror of some in the audience, I literally took
a pair of scissors and cut out these difficult passages. I suggested,
however, that those who choose which sections of scripture to
obey and which to disobey offend God far more than the physical cutting of a Bible.

*A "Christian" young man brought his non-Christian girl-
friend to camp. During the week, as she heard about who Jesus
is and His love for her, she gave her life to Christ. As she learned
about God's standards for sexual purity in relationships, she
asked a very disturbing question of her boyfriend. "You knew
all this?" He had not been following God's Word in relation to
its teaching on sexual purity.*

It is absolutely critical that you marry someone who believes
that God's Word is to be followed fully; otherwise, your spouse
becomes the absolute authority in right and wrong.

While this area of spiritual compatibility may be critical now, it will become even more so as you have children and need to agree on a standard by which to raise them.

Ask yourself whether your beloved's view of scripture governs his actions at work. Is he a man who acts with integrity even when his "boss" directs him to act otherwise? Is she willing to refuse to go to the movies with her friends because of the content of the movie, even if they make fun of her views?

Choose to marry only a person who loves God's Word, holds it as the highest authority, and seeks to understand it and live accordingly. And, if all of this is going to be true, one must *know* what scripture says. The only way to know what scripture says is to be a man or woman who regularly studies God's Word.

Making It Personal

- Have you seen your partner choose to follow God's Word, even when it may cost more financially?

- Does your partner obey God's Word even when his or her emotions are saying something different?

- Have you *both* relied on God's Word to set physical boundaries when hormones were raging?

- Have you observed the other choose to obey God's Word in family relationships and to extend forgiveness, even when having been wronged?

- Are you reading God's Word on a regular basis? Is your friend?

- Do you see God's Word affecting how you and your special friend live life?

Making It Plural

Jot down notes and discuss the areas this question confirmed for you or the issues that were raised in your mind which merit further discussion.

Circle the number that best represents how you feel about your relationship in light of The Word-of-God Question.

10	9	8	7	6	5	4	3	2	1

Extremely confident   ⟵——————⟶   Extremely hesitant

4 / The Completeness Question

Are you looking to marriage to make you complete?

Does the person you are attracted to seem fulfilled as a single? Does she seem to "need" you? Do you find yourself feeling "if only I were married, all my issues would be taken care of?"

"The two become one" is one of the greatest mysteries of scripture, and yet when understood and lived out it has the potential for the greatest delight. The mystery is that it is not two halves that become one, but two *wholes* that become one. The former is mathematics, the latter mystery.

Often, married couples talk about their "better half," implying that they in themselves are incomplete. There is some truth to that *after* marriage; but before marriage, it is two whole people that God joins together, not two half-persons.

I distinctly remember shopping for romantic cards to send to Virginia before we were married and being somewhat amused by the script on some of the cards: "The sun never shined before I met you", "The grass was always brown before I met you" (I'm talking about the kind you *mow*), "The birds never sang before I met you," etc. That simply was not true in our case; the sun did shine before I met Virginia, the grass was green, and the birds sang. I didn't marry Virginia because I was miserable; I married her because life with her promised to be even better than what I was enjoying now. In fact, one of the things that attracted me to Virginia was how hard it was to get time with her because she was so involved in life.

Now don't get me wrong: I think marriage is a blast and am so very glad I am married. But I do not worry that if something happened to me, Virginia could not survive. I trust she would miss me, but I know she does not need me to find meaning in life. If our worth, significance, and wholeness come from our mates, we have given them way too much power over us. They would then have the power to destroy us. If our significance, wholeness, and worth come from Christ, our spouses can hurt us deeply, but cannot destroy us.

In no way do I want to minimize the issue of loneliness for a single person, nor the God-given desire to be married. My concern is for when we expect marriage to meet deficits we have as singles. Colossians 2:10 teaches us that our completeness is to be found in Christ.

It would be humorous if it weren't so sad: many of the singles we counsel want to be married, and many of the married people we counsel want to be single.

A woman who marries to find completeness and meaning in life will find only disappointment and unmet expectations. She will soon realize that her insecurities and loneliness have only been magnified, because no partner is able to meet all those needs. Many of these women who marry poorly come to realize that even their best day of marriage is far worse than being single ever was.

When our girls were young, Virginia and I took them on what has become known as "the survival hike." As we were out driving together one day, we spontaneously decided to go on a hike. We did not count the costs of the extremely hot day or our lack of drinking water for the trip. After hiking a while, we were a bit thirsty. We came across a German couple who explained they had no water to offer us but would gladly share some of their beer. Our 12-year-old, Kari, was disgusted by the thought. We graciously declined their offer and continued hiking. After a few more hours of hiking without water Kari said, "If we see those

Germans again, I'm going to drink their beer!" When our needs are being met we are able to be more selective on options that come our way. But when we are desperate, we are more likely to take whatever comes along. Make sure your life is "full" as an individual so you are not desperate for whoever comes your way.

> *Susie was raised in a Christian home and had followed God's Word concerning relationships to the best of her ability. She wanted very badly to get married and truly believed she could never be fully happy or complete unless she were married. She "told God" she would play by His rules for the first 30 years of her life, but if He did not give her a nice Christian husband before she turned 30, she would go out and get a husband on her own, and she did: when she turned 30 and found herself still single, she "lowered her standards," dated anyone and everyone, and very quickly found a man who would marry her. She married a man that did not share her faith, came from a very different background, and ended up being very abusive . . . but she was married.*

In the movie *Cool Runnings,* there is a scene where the Jamaican bobsled team finds out that their coach had once cheated in the Olympics in order to win and later had the gold medal taken away from him. When they ask him why he did it, the coach replies, "I had to win. . . . when you make winning your whole life, you have to keep on winning, no matter what." And then, in a statement of reflection and instruction, he says, "A gold medal is a wonderful thing. But if you're not enough *without* it, you'll never be enough *with* it."

Remember, if you are not satisfied without marriage, you will likely not be satisfied with marriage.

Making It Personal

- Is your friend fully involved in life, work, church, and the lives of others?

- Does your friend seem to cling to you as if you were the only person desirable to be with?

- When you are at social events together, is your friend able to interact with others without you, or are you very needed?

- Is your friend jealous any time you are not together?

- Do you sometimes feel a bit smothered?

- When you are not together, is life miserable for you?

- Do you honestly feel you are waiting for marriage so your life can really start?

Making It Plural

Jot down notes and discuss the areas this question confirmed for you or the issues that were raised in your mind which merit further discussion.

Circle the number that best represents how you feel about your relationship in light of The Completeness Question.

10	9	8	7	6	5	4	3	2	1

Extremely confident   ⟵   ⟶   Extremely hesitant

5 / The Commitment Question

Are you entering marriage with a covenant or contract mindset?

When I was a boy I spent each night listening to the Los Angeles Dodgers baseball games. Each year I knew that Sandy Koufax would be pitching and Wally Moon would be in center field. In those years, most fathers started their careers and retired from the same company. The typewriter I started high school with was the same one I concluded University with eight years later.

Today, baseball players are traded the way I traded baseball cards. Having a job with the same company for over three or four years is rare. Computers are obsolete before you unpack them at home. We are living in a culture that believes you can always upgrade or trade up for a better player, job, computer, or spouse.

At a Valentine Dessert night, I once asked a table of couples who had been married an average of 52 years what their secret was. They shrugged their shoulders and said, "We made a commitment." Doesn't sound very romantic, but these couples were very much in love after 50 years together. One wife later confided in me that early in their marriage she was not happily married to her husband, but she had made a covenant commitment "until death do us part." She felt murder was wrong, so she stayed married. With a giant smile, she said, "I sure am glad I didn't leave him 40 years ago. He is the best dad and husband I can imagine."

45

I met with a lady in my office who had come to see the pastor to "get permission" to divorce. She told me she needed to get a divorce from her husband and wanted to do it in the least painful way possible. Since my practice is to attempt to bring healing to marriage, not to reduce the pain of divorce, I proceeded to ask her a series of questions.

"Has he been sexually unfaithful to you?"

"No."

"Has he physically, verbally, or emotionally abused you?"

"Oh, no."

"Has he failed to provide for you?"

"No, he is a wonderful provider."

"Is he an absent father?"

"No, actually that is the worst part—the kids will be devastated. They love him, and he is a wonderful dad."

"I am sorry," I said, "I guess I have missed something. Why is it you want a divorce?"

"Because he is *boring*," was her reply.

Our expectations for marriage, even in the Christian community, have become so high that it is virtually impossible for any marriage to meet the standards. I am all for striving for vital marriages. However, the basis for a marriage to stay together is first of all that it is a *covenant* relationship, not that it is necessarily an ideal relationship.

Many people get married with this thought in the backs of their minds: "If it doesn't work out, I can upgrade." Some people look at their parents and observe that they are still married even though they had problems; therefore these people assume they will attain the same success in their marriages. Unfortunately, we live in a culture today that constantly screams in our ears, "Don't you have the right to be happy?"

God has nothing against happiness, but *never* at the expense of obedience.

There are ways you are able to observe a "covenant" mentality before marriage. Whenever I hear someone talking about another's divorce, I have a pretty good view of his or her "covenant" mentality. When I hear phrases such as "well, they just weren't happy" or "he found someone who really is better suited for him" or "she just became much more educated than he was, and you can't expect her to stay married for the rest of her life to someone who is intellectually such a mis-match," I know the person is not a good prospect for a covenant marriage.

You can also observe how someone performs in a job, friendship, or church environment when desires and expectations are not being met. Marry someone who keeps a commitment, even when there are easier or more attractive options available.

Take a hard look at both of you and examine your level of commitment to each other: "For richer, for poorer; for better, for worse; in sickness and health . . . until *death* do us part." This is one of the reasons we encourage longer courtships. You need time to observe within yourselves your levels of commitment during the ups and downs of your relationship.

The tenth commandment is that we are not to covet what is not ours. In marriage, we are not to covet another partner. Once we start coveting what we don't have, we fail to work on—and be thankful for—what we do have.

Commitment is something you can observe in one another before marriage, and that is what will keep you together through the valleys and allow you to see the vistas together.

Making It Personal

- Does she keep her word to attend a function that she has committed to, even when a better offer has come up? Does he finish out his contract, even though he is unhappy in his position?

- Are her friends primarily those who have left marriages to pursue "greener pastures"?

- Is he still hanging out with single women who are his close friends? Is she still hanging out with single men who are her close friends?

- Does your partner tend to leave relationships when they become difficult?

- How does he/she react when told of a couple divorcing?

Making It Plural

Jot down notes and discuss the areas this question confirmed for you or the issues that were raised in your mind which merit further discussion.

Circle the number that best represents how you feel about your relationship in light of The Commitment Question.

10	9	8	7	6	5	4	3	2	1

Extremely confident   ⟵   ⟶   Extremely hesitant

Questions on
*C*haracter

6 / The Time Question

Has your relationship spanned four seasons?

We call it "the four-season rule." Have you each seen how the other one of you views and celebrates holidays, birthdays, football season, etc.? Often couples make lifelong decisions based on a very short exposure to one another. Give yourselves plenty of time to observe each other's true character throughout the seasons of the year.

Virginia was listening to a woman tell how she had found "the man of her dreams." She and her boyfriend of three months were talking of marriage and hoped to be married before too many more months passed—just enough time to plan the ceremony. He was everything she had ever hoped for, and so much different from the last man she had dated. After listening for a while, my wife mentioned that at the three-month mark, her former boy-friend was also "everything she had ever wanted." Yet by month six, the relationship had fallen apart.

Have you known each other long enough to see each other in situations that are out of the romantic setting and into the day-to-day grind? There is nothing magical about a year other than that during that length of time you are more likely to have the opportunity to accurately see each other in the "not-my-best" moments. In addition, during those twelve months you will be able to watch how the other celebrates each holiday, note how the other enjoys (or complains about) each of the four seasons (plus football season and hunting season!), see how the other spends vacation time, and observe the response to illness or any of the other challenges of life that naturally arise in a year's time.

A couple were married after a very short courtship. Her first married birthday was a bit of a shock for the young husband. He grew up in a family where birthdays were virtually ignored. She grew up in a family where you were "queen for the day." Her birthday arrived with great anticipation for the young bride but ended with many tears, largely due to the fact that he had no idea of her expectations for that day because he had never experienced a birthday with her prior to marriage.

In his first marriage, he had a pretty significant problem with anger and rage. He and his new fiancee sat in our office as they proudly announced that in their (short) courtship she had never seem him angry. But did she really believe she had seen enough to know his rage had vanished without a trace?

We actually suggest not making any life-long commitments prior to marking one year of friendship. While some couples may refrain from getting married before the year is up, many are already talking about marriage after only a few months—or they become engaged at the six-month mark. When commitments are made this quickly, the couple often starts "playing married" physically and/or emotionally. They shut down their critical-thinking mechanisms and go into the preparing-to-get-married stage. Far better to benefit from a full year of learning about each other and relating to each other without the distraction of marriage talk.

We often say to couples, "Time is your friend." If the relationship is meant to be, then waiting will not cause harm. Virginia often encourages couples to "enjoy the meadow," using an analogy that came to her as she and our daughter Kari were hiking in the Swiss Alps. They were walking through a flower-strewn meadow to arrive at the trail head that would take them to their destination for the day. In their excitement to climb the mountain, it was easy to miss the beautiful meadow they were crossing to get there. Similarly, in our relationships, it is possible to have our sights so set on "getting to the altar" that we forget to take our time and enjoy each day of the relationship.

If you have any sense that you are "securing the relationship" through engagement so that his or her options are shut down, you have made a great mistake. If a couple is truly meant to be together, time and even exposure to others will serve to confirm their love for each other. I remember vividly the gradual change that came over me while dating Virginia. Early in my dating experience, I would encounter a woman and think, "She could be interesting," or, "I could see myself with her." As time went on, such exposure was met with thoughts of "I am so glad I have Virginia; no one else compares with her."

Those who rush relationships—and especially commitments—often wonder later, "What might have been?"

Intentionally putting yourself in as many situations as possible with your potential spouse before you make the marriage decision is certainly a wise choice. Some may question the benefits of experiencing your first birthday celebration together prior to marriage rather than just toughing things out through your first year of marriage. They ask, "Why shouldn't we experience the benefits of marriage while we are getting to know each other more fully?" We would suggest that marriage itself has enough challenges without entering this relationship with additional unknowns. We have counseled far too many couples who, had they foreseen in their pre-married days what they experienced during their first year of marriage, would not have chosen to marry.

The first year of marriage should be a blast. In the words of Deuteronomy 24:5: "If a man has recently married, he must not be sent to war or have any other duty laid on him. For one year he is to be free to stay at home and bring happiness to the wife he has married."

The first year of marriage will tend to have a lot more happiness if you have cleared away as many responsibilities and unknowns as possible and can simply focus on each other.

Making It Personal

- Is there a sense of "rush" on either of your parts?

- Have you seen each other sick? tired? irritated?

- Have you spent holidays with each other's families?

- Have you experienced a birthday and observed the level of importance it plays in the other's life?

- Have you observed him during football, golf, baseball, and hunting seasons?

- Do you fear what more time might reveal about either of you?

Making It Plural

Jot down notes and discuss the areas this question confirmed for you or the issues that were raised in your mind which merit further discussion.

Circle the number that best represents how you feel about your relationship in light of The Time Question.

10	9	8	7	6	5	4	3	2	1

Extremely confident   ←——————→   Extremely hesitant

7 / *The Servanthood Question*

Is he/she interested in your needs above his/her own?

Our natural tendency is to look for a mate who is able to meet our needs. It is true that many of our needs will be met in marriage. However, if you get married because you are looking for someone else to serve you and to meet your needs, you will likely be very frustrated by your mate's inability to do this. On the other hand, if you marry so that you are able to meet the needs of that special someone, you will always have opportunities to do this.

> *Jim was an outgoing, talented musician who was the life of the party. He married Julie and treated her as royalty. After a number of years, Jim came down with multiple sclerosis and was no longer able to "meet Julie's needs." Before long, Julie left Jim for someone else who could "meet her needs."*

While you never know what life will send your way, it is possible to observe ahead of marriage whether your potential mate has a tendency toward preferring to be served, or instead seems to find great joy in serving others.

Selfishness can be seen in the routine of every day life—and that is where it is most often expressed in marriage as well.

> *It never struck her as odd that he always had to eat pizza when they went out, and he insisted on playing golf every*

weekend instead of doing an activity together. He was fun, popular, and successful, and everybody loved him. He did seem to be the first in line, to take the best piece of chicken, and to pick the biggest piece of dessert. But, hey, that's what made him successful—he was aggressive. After the babies, however, he continued to eat pizza, play golf, and generally put his desires ahead of everyone else's. But now the stakes are higher. Now they always go to his preferred vacation destinations and purchase his favorite cars.

Character is deep-seated. She will only go to "chick flicks" and gets moody when her wishes are not always met. He feels like he is always hoping to "get it right" so she won't be upset with his lack of care and attention to her needs.

Forestine and Claude have been two of our dearest friends. During one visit with us, Forestine, in the mid stages of Alzheimer's, retold the same story every four or five minutes without ridicule from Claude. Afterwards, as Claude and I made our way to the car while Virginia and Forestine finished up their conversation, I commented to Claude on how hard her condition must be on him. But he simply replied, "Forestine has been such a servant to me all these years; now I have the privilege of serving her by caring for her during this season of her life."

Look for ways your friend serves others even when it's an inconvenience or there is nothing to be received in return. This is the person you will want to grow old with.

Making It Personal

- Do you see this special friend finding joy in serving others?

- Is she upset if those who are served do not reciprocate?

- Does he tend to put his desires first when it comes to time you spend together?

- When a project gets tough, does he tend to walk away?

- Is he upset with others when they get ahead of him in line?

- Does she tend to give others the best seats or rush to have them for herself?

- Does he care for the needy or only those who "have it together?"

- Is serving an event or a lifestyle?

Making It Plural

Jot down notes and discuss the areas this question confirmed for you or the issues that were raised in your mind which merit further discussion.

Circle the number that best represents how you feel about your relationship in light of The Servanthood Question.

10	9	8	7	6	5	4	3	2	1

Extremely confident   ⟵⟶   Extremely hesitant

8 / The Parents Question

What role will your future in-laws likely play in your marriage?

The saying goes that in reality, you are not marrying a person, you are marrying a family. Although couples marry each other, they often overlook the significant part that "parental blessing" plays in a satisfying marriage.

Sally's family frankly didn't think George was good enough for their little girl. Sally came from a close family and felt torn by their opinion of her relationship. George appreciated the closeness of Sally's family and in no way wanted to create tension. On the other hand, he was not willing to let Sally go. George made the decision that because of his love for Sally and his admiration for her family, he would continue to date Sally but wait for the parents' approval. It took three years, but Sally and George walked down the aisle with everyone's blessing.

In cases where your family shares your values and you have had a close relationship with them, it is especially important to listen to their observations. If you feel they "don't really know" your potential partner, give them time and provide opportunities for them to get to know him or her. It is much better to wait a bit longer to get married and marry with your family's blessing than to rush headstrong into marriage without their blessing. For some, these "parents" may be extended family or friends who have become "chosen family."

In cases where you may be a Christian and your parents are not, or where you have significantly differing values (for example, your parents wanted you to marry a doctor or a high-powered and wealthy business person, but you have been attracted to someone who shares your passion for missions and reaching the lost), again, take time! Try to help your parents see your heart and your plan—then go ahead, realizing that you may truly be choosing your future spouse at the expense of (at least temporarily) a close relationship with your family.

The first step to marital oneness is to leave your mother and father. You can cleave to your spouse only to the degree you have left your parents. The Hebrew word for "leave" means "to cut, sever, or abandon." This does not mean to separate relationally from one's parents, but it does mean to switch one's primary allegiance from one's parents. A married man is now one with his wife, not one with his parents (Genesis 2:24). Parents are given the responsibility to raise a child with the expectation that their child will one day leave them and form a new relationship with a spouse.

Many will say, "We're just adding another setting to the Sunday dinner table," or, "You're not losing a son, you're gaining a daughter!" The Biblical reality is that parents of a newlywed groom are taking a place setting away from the Sunday table and are losing a son, not gaining a daughter.

Each newly married couple should be free to start their own traditions and make their own plans. If they choose to spend holidays with their families, that's fine; but it is their choice, not their parents' choice. Your allegiance will be to your spouse and to his or her needs first—not your parents. This may sound harsh, and you may ask, "Can't I please serve both?" The answer is "yes, sometimes." Certainly a couple will want to maintain healthy relationships with their extended families, but that will happen only when both husband and wife are secure in the knowledge that each is the highest priority relationship for the other.

A newly married couple was expecting the groom's parents up for the weekend. One area of tension already was the mother's calls questioning whether or not the new bride was able to prepare the favorite dishes her son liked so much. The wise son, not wanting to subject his wife's cooking to his mother's scrutiny, told his parents that they would be going out for dinner on Saturday night to an Italian restaurant that he and his wife liked very much. The young couple had an engagement during Saturday afternoon but assured the parents they would be home in time to go to dinner. When the young couple arrived home, the aroma of the groom's mother's home-cooked meal greeted them. When the groom questioned his mother about what was going on, she said, "I knew you must have been missing my home-cooked meals. I fixed you your favorite meal, so we can eat at home tonight." The young husband immediately said, "That's wonderful, Mom. We can put it in the refrigerator and have it tomorrow, because tonight we are going out to dinner as we had said." Many sons would turn to their wives at this point and say, "Look at all the work Mom has gone to—let's cancel our reservation, eat at home, and go out tomorrow." Not this son. He saw exactly what was happening and aligned himself with his bride. His bride later commented, "At the point he said, 'We are going out to dinner,' I realized he had truly left home and was choosing to be one with me." (paraphrased from *The Seven Principles for Making Marriage Work* by John M. Gottman)

This is an especially difficult concept in some cultures where honor and obedience are seen as synonymous, and going against the wishes and commands of your parents is seen as disgracing them. While we are always to be sensitive to culture, if scripture and culture contradict each other, we are always called to obey scripture.

When we marry, we need to be willing to move our primary allegiance from our parents to our spouse. Such a decision should not be entered into lightly.

Making It Personal

- Take note of the expectations your friend's parents have for their child's future spouse.

- Work on showing your future in-laws that you will be a great spouse rather than resenting their concern for their child.

- Is your potential mate presently dependent on his parents for financial assistance?

- When it comes to decision-making, what role do your future in-laws play?

- What are their holiday expectations after marriage for your new family?

- Have you seen ways in which your future mate has left or is preparing to leave home behind?

- Does your future mate know that some of the holiday traditions may change once you are married?

- What are the expectations surrounding your attendance at extended family vacations?

- To what degree do you see pleasing the parents as a very high priority for your fiancé?

Making It Plural

Jot down notes and discuss the areas this question confirmed for you or the issues that were raised in your mind which merit further discussion.

Circle the number that best represents how you feel about your relationship in light of The Parents Question.

10   9   8   7   6   5   4   3   2   1

Extremely confident   ←————————→   Extremely hesitant

9 / The Respect Question

Is she willing to respect you and submit to your leadership?

Men, this one is primarily for you. An engaged woman, talking about her parents, said, "My father is the head of our home. My mother is the neck that turns the head."

Although this may get a laugh, it is, unfortunately, not a laughing matter in many homes where the husband does not feel respected.

Virginia and I had six couples over for dinner and were discussing what husbands and wives wished their spouses understood about them. The men agreed unanimously: "We wish our wives understood how important it is for them to respect us." Most men would say that having a wife that respects them is more important than virtually anything else.

The tendency in "daughters of Eve" is to control their husbands, leaving men feel less than respected. In Genesis 3:16, God addresses Eve and says, "Your desire will be for your husband, and he will rule over you." As used in this verse, the word "desire" means a desire to control. It is interesting that because of the fall, women will tend to control their husbands and husbands will attempt to rule over their wives. In Ephesians 5, women are commanded to respect their husbands and husbands are commanded to love their wives. Ephesians 5 is the antidote to the fall. But don't miss the point: women's tendency leads them away from respect for their husbands.

Men, let me be very clear: you should not be looking for a woman who will not challenge you and cause you to grow. But I assure you, you do not want to be married to a woman who belittles you, corrects you, and overrides you.

I met recently with a couple where the man said his wife does not show respect to him. He said that when he comes home at night, she calls him "stupid" or "an idiot." When I asked her if that were true, she said, "Yes, but I wouldn't need to call him an idiot if he did things correctly." This woman not only wore the pants in the family, she carried the rifle as well. This man was a shell of what he might have been had he been married to a supportive wife.

Some clues before marriage would be: Does she often correct you? Does she let you know that whatever you do is not quite good enough? Does she override your decisions or make them for you?

Is she a woman from whom you feel respect? Or do you find yourself often "yielding" to her demands? Does she seem to want to control you and the relationship?

You can often see this in observing not only her relationship with you, but with others as well. Do you observe her overruling you and others? Often women step in and lead because of the void left by weak men. So the challenge is certainly to men to lead, but be wary of a woman who overrules you so that you end up following rather than leading.

At a counseling session, the husband opened by saying that he felt unwanted, unnecessary, and unappreciated in his home. He said, "Whatever I say will be confirmed or overruled by my wife. I feel as if I really am unnecessary." The wife joined in and said, "I realize I am partially to blame. I married a strong man and have whittled him down over the years with corrections, directives, and negative statements. I took over control and did not let him lead, and now I hate him for it. I now realize I was involved in the process that contributed to his passivity."

In an attempt to bring some humor to a gathering, a man who had been married six months was asked, "What is the secret to being married successfully for six months?" His answer drew a laugh, but it was not funny: He said, "I have learned to say 'Yes, dear.'"

There are far too many Christian men in their 60s or 70s who have become "Yes, dear" men. In order to avoid conflict, they simply go along with the demands of their wives, and continue to lose respect as they do so.

Men, make sure you marry a woman who respects you as a leader, and interacts with you but doesn't overrule you. Remember, you are able to choose the one who will either respect you or not before you are married. Marry a woman who respects you and builds you up. You will never regret it.

Making It Personal

- Does she need to be right and/or "win" discussions?

- Do you feel she overrides your decisions at times?

- Have you ever felt she treats you as a child?

- Do you try hard to please her only to feel like you have fallen short?

- Does she affirm you in private and in public?

- How do the two of you make decisions?

- Do you tend to default into a "yes, dear" mode in order to keep peace in the relationship?

Making It Plural

Jot down notes and discuss the areas this question confirmed for you or the issues that were raised in your mind which merit further discussion.

Circle the number that best represents how you feel about your relationship in light of The Respect Question.

10	9	8	7	6	5	4	3	2	1

Extremely confident ←――――――→ Extremely hesitant

Do you feel loved and cherished by him?

This question is especially directed toward the women. Do you feel loved and cherished by your boyfriend? Does he make you feel like a princess? Does he love to discover what is important to you and then help to make it happen? Or does he seem to make fun of you and ridicule those "silly things" that seem so important to you? Does he seem genuinely interested in serving you and putting your needs ahead of his own?

As you read this set of emails from a woman who is feeling cherished, ask yourself, "Is that how I am feeling?" It should be.

George is such a godly man and I have been truly inspired by him to grow closer to God during these months we have spent together. His discipline to go to God and his desire to bathe in God's Word is such a gift to me. I still can't believe I have done this before any other way. It reminds me of how great Satan is at convincing us otherwise—that old—"Surely God won't mind if you just . . ." God does mind, and what is worse at the human level is what it does to us in the process. I am getting to know George for the person he is and he is getting to know me. We are doing things we can tell others about without having to feel ashamed or guilty for it.

I am so blessed by the fact that George has taken the lead in this and kept us faithful! For once, a man with strong convictions—

what a blessing!! Phew! It makes such a difference in our ability to see clearly and get to know one another for who we are without the blinders that the physical relationship brings. This to me is the greatest gift of all.

George proposed to me today at about noon!!! It was the most romantic and wonderful time of my life, without a doubt. He staged the whole thing beautifully with God's amazing help and blessing in that it happened to be a most beautiful day—blue skies and great temps. We hiked up to the mountain near his home for a "short walk". When we arrived at the location of our first date, on the chair lift platform, George read to me the most beautiful proposal and proceeded to get on his knee and ask me to marry him! Of course I gladly accepted! He proceeded to bring out the CD player with swing music and we danced a few numbers! Then he brought out a table and folding chairs, tablecloth, roses, and champagne! He served strawberries as our first course, shrimp as the main course, and chocolate ice cream for dessert! It was absolutely a dream come true!

Did you notice in her description of George that she referred to his godliness and that it had inspired her to grow closer to God herself? According to Ephesians 5, one of the ways a man cherishes his wife is to help her grow spiritually. Would you say that since you started dating, your relationship with the Lord has deepened? You want a man who encourages and inspires you to grow.

In the account of the proposal, it is obvious that George knew his fiancée and created a proposal that would meet her desires and dreams. I have far too often seen men propose in a way that meets *their* desires and dreams but does not take into account the temperament and desires of their girlfriends. For instance, an extraverted man plans a huge engagement party to follow his proposal—but if his fiancée is an introvert, she would likely prefer a quiet evening alone with her fiancé over a party with friends.

Part of the challenge to every husband in Ephesians 5 is to make his wife more radiant (verse 25). Will your fiancé delight in helping you realize your dreams, desires, abilities, and gifts, or do you see him expecting you to put your dreams on the shelf in order for him to realize his dreams? Godly husbands know their spouses and delight in helping them to become all God designed them to be.

Complaints we frequently hear from women are "I don't feel cherished by him" and "He doesn't even seem to know me" and "Just once, I would like to feel more important than his work." Next to his relationship with the Lord, you should be number one. Do you feel so now? If not, the likelihood of you becoming number one in his life after marriage is slim.

How is he doing as a servant leader? One of the greatest complaints we hear from wives is "He doesn't lead!" Or "He seldom takes initiative." Some men believe they are being servants when in reality they are shirking their leadership responsibilities. It's not uncommon for married men to develop a "whatever you wish, dear" mentality, counting on this to avoid conflict and allow the wife to do what she wishes. Women tell us that all that does is to make them feel responsible for the decisions. It's like the cartoon in which the husband states that he makes all the big decisions in life and his wife makes all the little ones—and thus far there have been no big decisions.

Practically, this could be illustrated by the following scenario. A husband comes home from work and asks, "What's up for dinner?" The wife says, "Sorry, nothing is ready. I've had a rough day." The husband says, "Well, do whatever you want for dinner; let's just make a decision so I don't miss the start of Monday Night Football."

Not only does she not feel cared for, she also feels all the pressure to lead. A better scenario: the husband comes home and senses his wife has had a rough day. "Why don't we go out tonight and grab a bite to eat at that new Mexican restaurant on

5th Street?" The wife says, "You know, I just ate there yesterday with some of my friends and it wasn't that great. How about our favorite Chinese place by the high school?"

"That sounds good. Let's go," replies the husband.

In the second scenario, he is still interested in serving her by letting her choose the restaurant, yet he has taken initiative. Women state that this makes all the difference in the world.

A single woman recently sent us an email that addresses this subject:

> I just felt like he didn't take charge of the date, and that was a bit of a turnoff. It was kind of an aimless date. We didn't know where we were going to eat and we ended up watching a movie I had rented at my place . . . I guess for me, a man taking charge of the night represents the difference between a platonic and a romantic evening.

Do you respect him? Specifically, scripture commands women to submit to and respect their husbands. Women, is this man the man whom you wish to submit to and choose to respect for the rest of your life? Is he one with whom you will joyfully partner? Does he exhibit the kind of sacrificial, caring leadership that will make you feel loved and cherished?

Making It Personal

- Do you feel like a princess when you are with your boyfriend?

- Does he take the lead in protecting you in your physical relationship?

- Is he romantic?

- Does he put your interests and preferences ahead of his own?

- Are you becoming more like who you want to be because of him?

- When he comes over, does he simply plop himself down and wait for you to suggest what to do?

- Is he creative enough to take the initiative to surprise you with a specially planned night out?

- Do you feel he respects your opinions, and yet does not automatically yield to them?

- Does this man lead in a way you respect?

- Does this man lead in a way that makes you feel loved?

Making It Plural

Jot down notes and discuss the areas this question confirmed for you or the issues that were raised in your mind which merit further discussion.

Circle the number that best represents how you feel about your relationship in light of The Cherishing Question.

10	9	8	7	6	5	4	3	2	1

Extremely confident ⟵⟶ Extremely hesitant

11 / The Provision Question

Is he going to be able to provide for you?

Many women who come from homes with absent, unaffectionate, or driven fathers find themselves attracted to men who are available to them, affirming, and affectionate, rather than driven by the "things of the world." Later, these women often complain that their husbands don't lead or take initiative. The wife soon discovers that the reason he was always available was because he never *did* anything. That may be flattering during the dating period, but it quickly becomes old during marriage. Ask yourself if he is a man who has the strength to lead and provide for you and your family in ways that honor God and honor you.

Lisa was an attorney; Alan was a security guard. They became engaged three months after they met. Not long after the engagement announcement, he was fired from his job as a security guard because he showed up late so often and occasionally fell asleep on the job. He told Lisa that he was fired due to the stress of the upcoming wedding and that after they were married he would get another job, but that it didn't make sense to get a new job three months before the wedding and honeymoon. Fast-forward eight years. Alan is still hoping to get a job. He now stays home with their 4-year-old boy, but finds child-rearing quite draining. Lisa works a full-time job and then comes home to clean house, cook, and take care of their son for the evening since Alan has watched him all day.

It seems elementary, but: "no money, no honey." Postpone the wedding if necessary, but don't get married without the groom having had a stable job for at least a year.

I certainly am not saying that women can't work outside the home. What I want to encourage is that a husband not become dependent on his wife as the primary provider. Some may argue that the man can be a stay-at-home dad. There are certainly specific circumstances such as health reasons or "stage of life" that can necessitate the wife becoming the primary salary earner for a season. But it seems to Virginia and me that God has wired men to be primary providers and women to be primary nurturers. That does not mean that men are not able to nurture and women are not able to provide, but it is typically not our strongest natural wiring.

Look at your potential husband's work history closely. If he did not have a good work ethic and job record before you met, don't count on them after you marry. Be realistic about what life will be like with someone who does not provide well. I am not talking about riches, I am talking about provision. Many women get married thinking, "We will live on love." Think instead about the fact that utility companies, supermarkets, and apartment complexes may take a Visa card, but not the "love" card.

Some men spiritualize it. "God will provide," they'll say, or "We just need to trust God more." Although these statements are true, they do not lessen the responsibility of a husband to be a provider. As we read in 2 Thessalonians 3:10, "If a man will not work, he shall not eat," and in 1 Timothy 5:8, "If anyone does not provide for his relatives, and especially for his immediate family, he has denied the faith and is worse than an unbeliever."

A couple came in for counseling. The husband's gross income for the previous year was $11,000. The wife, an accomplished executive secretary, made the money that truly provided for the *family's necessary income and benefits. In order for them to be able to start a family and allow her to stay home to care for children, he will need to become the primary provider. They are still childless.*

Make sure you marry a man who is able to provide financially for you.

Making It Personal

- What has his job record been for the last five years?

- When you go out together, who pays?

- If he gets laid off, what does he do to seek reemployment?

- Has he taken on temporary work that may be "beneath" him, or does he continue to wait for the perfect job "to which he has become accustomed"?

- What size savings account does he have?

- How much debt is he carrying?

- How is he going to pay for the honeymoon?

- What potential do you see in being able to live on his salary alone if children come along?

Making It Plural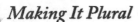

Jot down notes and discuss the areas this question confirmed for you or the issues that were raised in your mind which merit further discussion.

Circle the number that best represents how you feel about your relationship in light of The Provision Question.

10	9	8	7	6	5	4	3	2	1

Extremely confident   ⟵——————⟶   Extremely hesitant

What sort of parent will your date make?

Today, more and more couples are opting not to have children. Talk honestly about this. Whether or not to have children is a huge decision, and the importance of full disclosure and honesty with each other about this question is critical. And even if your future mate claims to be fine with children, observe how he or she interacts with and talks about children.

Your special friend may make a fun date, and may even make a good spouse—but will this person make a good parent for your children? Look for someone who will model for your children the values to which you are committed. Marry a person who will be willing to put the needs of your children ahead of self: ahead of interests, hobbies, and work. Again, a good indicator is to watch how he or she interacts with children and talks about children, and how children were cared for in his or her family of origin.

The only thing you will have together that will truly outlast you will be your children. As you choose a husband or wife, you are choosing the person who will shape your children.

Bob sat in the counseling office. "I have a great job, a beautiful wife, and two terrific kids, but I am tired of being a dad. I would much rather hang out at the bar with my friends than at home with my girls. Do you think I'm selfish?"

Bingo! Guys who are fun to date do not necessarily make great dads. Women who are a blast to be with don't necessarily make great moms.

Listen closely to how he talks about children: does he speak of parents putting children in childcare, the way children limit a couple's freedom, and so on? I remember hearing a couple who were contemplating children say, "One thing's for sure: a child will not interrupt the lifestyle and activities we have enjoyed." Think again . . .

> *A couple was arguing in the counselors' office about whether to divorce. The man complained that his wife was no longer the woman he married. "You used to go out clubbing and come in at 2 am. Now you stay at home!" Her retort was, "I'm changing diapers now at 2 am. Life changes—grow up!"*

What sort of personal morals and values do you expect your future spouse to model for your children?

One of the strongest statements about children in scripture comes from Jesus, who said (as recorded in Mark 9:42), "And if anyone causes one of these little ones who believe in me to sin, it would be better for him to be thrown into the sea with a large millstone tied around his neck." The role of a parent in a child's spiritual development is critical. Make certain that the mother or father of your children *helps* and does not hinder your children's desire to follow Christ.

For the vast majority of marriages, children will come into the picture at some point. Make sure you marry someone who has the character and values you want imitated. I gave a framed picture of our three daughters to Virginia on her 45th birthday. The caption reads, "These apples didn't fall far from the tree . . . Thanks for being such a great tree."

Take a good look at the tree, because the tree produces the fruit.

Making It Personal

- How have you seen your potential spouse play with children?

- What offhand remarks has he or she made about others' babies?

- Are the characteristics and values of your potential mate those you wish for your children?

- Do you see the other's "work ethic" being such that he or she will expend the energy needed to parent?

Making It Plural

Jot down notes and discuss the areas this question confirmed for you or the issues that were raised in your mind which merit further discussion.

Circle the number that best represents how you feel about your relationship in light of The Mother/Father Question.

10	9	8	7	6	5	4	3	2	1

Extremely confident   ⟵――――――⟶   Extremely hesitant

How satisfied are you with your communication?

How would you rate your verbal communication on a scale of 1 to 10? How do you make decisions? Do you have conflict? How do you handle conflict?

Jim and Joan sat in the counseling office on the brink of divorce. "He yells at me all the time. I can't even think when he gets angry, let alone communicate effectively."

"She won't talk, she just cowers. She lives in this fairy tale world where everyone has the same opinion and there are no disagreements."

"It is not a fairy tale: I grew up in that house—where we never yelled at each other."

"Yelled at? I raise my voice a little and she accuses me of yelling! Come live in the house I grew up in and you will see what yelling is. But we communicated, got it out, and moved on."

How communication and conflict were dealt with in our families of origin often shapes how we deal with conflicts in marriage. I grew up in a home where anger was not tolerated; Virginia grew up in a home with more freedom of verbal expression. When we had our first disagreement in our marriage, I thought our marriage was over. I had never seen conflict between my parents. Both of our families were strong Christian families; they just dealt with communication and conflict in a different way.

Anger is increasingly an issue in marriages. Make sure you are not marrying an angry man or woman. The anger you observe may currently be directed to "those idiots," but be assured that after marriage, you will become one of "those idiots." At some point, you will be treated similarly.

Ephesians 4:29 says, "Do not let any unwholesome talk come out of your mouths, but only what is helpful for building others up according to their needs, that it may benefit those who listen." Would you say your communication with each other is helpful or hurtful? Do you feel built up by the conversations, or torn down? Do you feel your date is sensitive to what you need in communication? Does his or her talk benefit those who listen?

> *At a counseling session, a husband verbally sliced and diced his wife. Her opinion was "wrong," she didn't think logically, she was too emotional. The wife cowered and would not enter into the dialogue. When pressed, she said she was trying to "get her ducks in a row" before speaking, but he always came out shooting her ducks before they were "in a row."*

Communication in marriage is vital to the health of a marriage. Make sure you are free with each other conversationally. Don't excuse each other by saying things like "He is only rude when he is under pressure" or "I am sure she won't sulk after we are married."

When my father was a young adult, he drove 400 miles to surprise his serious girlfriend, whom he planned to marry. As he walked up to the house, he heard his girlfriend screaming at her mother and treating her in a rude and disrespectful manner. He turned around, drove back home, and ended the relationship. He made his decision based on what he had observed about how this girl communicated with those she "loved." Such "love" was not the kind he was looking for, and he was sure there would be plenty of days when he would "tick her off." He simply didn't want to be on the receiving end of such destructive behavior.

There is no portion of scripture that deals as concisely with communication and conflict than Ephesians 4:25–32:

> Therefore each of you must put off falsehood and speak truthfully to his neighbor, for we are all members of one body. "In your anger do not sin": Do not let the sun go down while you are still angry, and do not give the devil a foothold. He who has been stealing must steal no longer, but must work, doing something useful with his own hands that he may have something to share with those in need.
>
> Do not let any unwholesome talk come out of your mouths, but only what is helpful for building others up according to their needs, that it may benefit those who listen. And do not grieve the Holy Spirit of God, with whom you were sealed for the day of redemption. Get rid of all bitterness, rage and anger, brawling and slander, along with every form of malice. Be kind and compassionate to one another, forgiving each other, just as in Christ God forgave you.

These eight verses challenge us to:
- be truthful
- handle anger without sinful destructive behavior
- deal with conflict quickly, honestly, and truthfully
- communicate wholesomely
- communicate in ways that build up
- communicate so as to benefit those who listen
- reject bitterness, rage, slander, and malice
- interact with compassion
- have a forgiving spirit

Be and look for someone with these healthy communication traits. If your future spouse doesn't have them now, he or she will not likely grow into them. Make sure you are marrying a person who uses communication in a constructive rather than destructive manner.

Making It Personal

- When driving, does your potential mate ever get angry?

- Does your friend refuse to enter into discussions where people have strong opinions and are willing to express them?

- When you are alone for long periods of time, are you able to communicate, or does silence or tension reign?

- How have you observed the other treating those at the checkout counter who seem incompetent?

- How does the other resolve conflict with friends?

- How does your friend communicate with his or her family?

- How do the two of you come to a decision when you disagree?

- Does one of you find yourself yielding to the other, just to keep peace?

- Do you find yourself saying too regularly, "It really doesn't matter to me—it's not worth any tension"?

- Is it important for one of you to be "right" in disagreements?

Making It Plural

Jot down notes and discuss the areas this question confirmed for you or the issues that were raised in your mind which merit further discussion.

Circle the number that best represents how you feel about your relationship in light of The Communication and Conflict Question.

10	9	8	7	6	5	4	3	2	1

Extremely confident   ⟵——————⟶   Extremely hesitant

Questions on
*C*ompatibility

14 / The Compatibility Question

Do you have a significant number of similar interests?

Are you both outdoors people, or both readers, or both physically active? Are your TV-watching habits similar? Compatibility is not what marriages are built on, but without a reasonable amount of it, marriages tend to stagnate.

Shelly was an avid outdoors enthusiast. She loved hiking, biking, skiing, you name it—if it was outdoors and required physical exertion, she was all over it. Steve had often gone camping with groups that included Shelly. In fact, the two of them participated in a few difficult hiking trips together. When Shelly announced her engagement, Steve was a bit surprised, since he knew her fiancé was pretty much a computer nerd who liked to stay indoors and work on his computer. Steve challenged Shelly about her choice for marriage and their seeming lack of common interests. She assured him they had talked it over and were both comfortable with who the other one was. A few months after marriage, Steve received a phone call from his now-married former hiking buddy Shelly. She said she had heard of a great three-day hike and wondered if he would like to go with her since her husband was not interested. Steve wisely declined, but the point was not lost. She was now looking for other companions to fill her desire for shared common interests.

Nowadays it is not uncommon to see such a couple get married. They don't see any need to give up their individual interests just because they are getting married. They assume that they can both pursue their passions outside of the marriage relationship; after all, they didn't lose their individual identities just because they got married, did they?

Such thinking sounds chic, modern, and mature, and yet it is extremely dangerous. The probability is high that someday, somewhere in an outdoor club, this young lady will find a guy, other than her husband, with whom she connects. She and her new friend will talk about all their common passions, and then she will mention how difficult it is to be married to someone who does not share these passions. Before long, they are not hiking with the club, but with each other . . . and the sad story ends in divorce. When Jesus was asked about divorce, he said, "'For this reason a man will leave his father and mother and be united to his wife, and the two will become one flesh.' So they are no longer two, but one. Therefore what God has joined together, let man not separate." (Matthew 19:5–6) Certainly Jesus does not mean that those who marry lose their individual gifts, talents, personalities, and passions—but it does follow from His teaching that these must be willingly sacrificed if they cause separation or lack of unity in the marriage.

Temperaments are another area worthy of study when it comes to compatibility. There are many different ways to measure temperament or personality, and a couple would be wise to have a professional choose one to review with them, such as the Myers-Briggs Type Indicator. Knowledge of how you are wired temperamentally can be of enormous help to both of you as you consider marriage.

I certainly do not mean to imply that a couple must share all the same passions, temperaments, and hobbies. But you must have enough in common that your friendship will continue to grow throughout your years of marriage together, and that you can each be confident the other does not secretly resent having been kept from fulfilling their dreams.

In the book *Date or Soul Mate: How to Know If Someone Is Worth Pursuing in Two Dates or Less*, author Neil Clark Warren makes the helpful observation that it is of critical importance to know what you can't live with and what you can't live without. For instance, the "hiker" mentioned earlier would have been wise to admit, "I can't live without sharing the outdoors with my spouse." Someone else might decide, "I can't live with someone who is obsessed with sports." You and your future spouse don't need to have all the same interests to be compatible, but those you are passionate about should be shared. You need enough common ground to stand on to make your relationship stable.

Making It Personal

- What interests did you each have before you met each other?

- What level of passion is there in the areas you don't share?

- Do you see your areas of compatibility drawing you closer together or pushing you apart?

- Does it seem that one of you has to make most of the effort to become "compatible" with the other?

- Do your temperaments seem to mesh together nicely or cause friction?

Making It Plural

Jot down notes and discuss the areas this question confirmed for you or the issues that were raised in your mind which merit further discussion.

Circle the number that best represents how you feel about your relationship in light of The Compatibility Question.

10   9   8   7   6   5   4   3   2   1

Extremely confident   ⟵ ⟶   Extremely hesitant

15 / The Motivation Question

Are you similar in the areas of motivation and accomplishment?

Motivation, or drive, is another important area in which to assess compatibility.

A young couple had been dating for two years when they broke off their relationship. They loved the Lord, served in Christian ministry, and guarded their physical and emotional intimacy, yet the man decided it was not a good fit. The area of compatibility that was lacking was "drive," "initiative," "motivation," and "direction." She was graduating from the university in three years while he was on the six- or seven-year plan. She knew what he wanted to do with her life, but he didn't have a clue.

Gerry and Sue lived in a small condo. Sue was a go-get-it sort of gal. She worked full time and did all the cooking, finances, and planning for the family. Gerry was offered various promotions at work but turned them all down, even though the commensurate pay would enable a significant move up in housing. He stayed at the same place in the company because he didn't want the additional responsibility and stress that would come with the promotion. Instead he came home each day and watched TV. They remained stuck in their condo and eventually stuck in their marriage.

This motivation thing is big! It is often overlooked because the "laid back" one brings balance to the "driven" one while the driven one gets things done for the laid-back one. The problem is that often as the marriage progresses there gradually develops great tension between the goals each spouse has. The motivated one may want to work hard to save and buy a house, while the laid-back one is happy to work fewer hours, relax more, and rent.

I remember once being on a very tight time schedule to catch a flight. As I started to run, mentally preparing myself to ask for "cuts" because our flight was about to depart, my friend said, "Hey, why rush? We're going to miss it anyway."

"Not without a fight, we're not," I said as I took off running. We did make the flight instead of being stuck for a night in an airport. I can't imagine being happily married to someone I was always having to "pull along."

This shows itself in simple things, such as experiencing new things when you travel versus "sleeping in" because you are tired and then missing many new sights and experiences.

If you are the laid-back one, it may seem exhausting to think of spending the rest of your life running to "see" and "accomplish." You would do well to marry someone who relaxes, enjoys the moment, and is not always pushing you.

You can often identify this trait by observing how the person approaches work. Is he working for a promotion, better education, or new experiences, or is he satisfied to stay with the status quo and not look to new vistas?

This issue of motivation can cause tension if either husband or wife is more motivated, but it seems to cause more tension when the wife is the more motivated one. It is easy for her to "push" her husband to be or accomplish more than he desires. This often ends up feeling to him like he is being nagged, when she is just trying to help her husband accomplish more. In the marketplace, when a man is criticized or fails, he may indeed work harder. But in the home, when his wife criticizes him or implies he is always wrong or inadequate, he quits and in essence says, "Fine, you do it!" Slowly, he becomes disengaged and aloof. He follows his wife's lead, and in the end, they resent each other for it.

Too many gifted women marry men who are nice enough, but have no vision, drive, or initiative. Too many men marry women who do not share their motivation and passion for excellence. Whether you tend to be highly motivated or the more laid-back type, it is much better to marry someone of a similar outlook than to feel pushed or pulled for the rest of your life.

Making It Personal

- How do the two of you compare when it comes to drive, motivation, or initiative?

- When projects become difficult, does your potential mate quit, or push through?

- Would you call your friend someone who really gives it his or her all, or just "gets through"?

- When it came to grades in school, did your future spouse excel to his or her best ability?

Making It Plural

Jot down notes and discuss the areas this question confirmed for you or the issues that were raised in your mind which merit further discussion.

Circle the number that best represents how you feel about your relationship in light of The Motivation Question.

10   9   8   7   6   5   4   3   2   1

Extremely confident   ⟵――――⟶   Extremely hesitant

How alike or different are your families of origin?

It doesn't hurt to take a good long look at your potential spouse's family of origin. Do you share a similar social status, ethnic background, and educational experience? Do your families have similar ways of handling conflict, money, vacations, or discretionary time? Would they enjoy vacationing together? While these are not necessarily make-or-break issues, they are definitely worth examining. Experience has proven that to a large extent, we are products of our families.

Linda graduated number one in her class from a prestigious university. Josh also graduated—barely. She could get a job anywhere she wanted; he wanted to get a job anywhere. She came from a wealthy, successful businessman's family. His family worked in menial jobs. Her family lived in the expensive part of town. His lived in the low-rent district. Linda's parents were cordial to their new son-in-law, but from the start, Josh didn't have much of a chance. He had certainly married up, and she had married down. Since her family was the more successful, better educated, and closer relationally, they would always keep her family's traditions and follow her family's way of doing something.

It is amazing how much we bring to a marriage from our families, even though we may not realize it. We may not have had the best childhood, but our parents will always be our parents and we want them to be proud of us, to like our spouse, and to think our decisions are good.

Some of these issues are extremely minor, while others may play a major role in our marriage relationship.

When our daughter Kari and her husband Gabe came home from their first time grocery shopping together, Kari started to put the bag of potatoes under the sink. Gabe exclaimed, "who puts their potatoes under the sink?" to which Kari responded, "my *mother*!"

We laugh about this, but realize that even *where the potatoes go* is affected by how life was lived in our childhood home. Other, bigger issues may be how the husband and wife sort out their domestic roles in the home and with the children. Bill Hybels tells the story of calling his wife Lynn to inform her where *he* was going on his vacation. His father had gone on many vacations without his wife or family. Lynn's father had never been away from his wife for even a night.

These are not issues of right and wrong, but are worth examining carefully because they affect your family decisions—such as how to spend holidays, with whom to spend holidays, how to celebrate birthdays, etc. The amount of tension created in establishing your own traditions is often proportional to the differences between your families of origin.

Differences in family backgrounds do not spell doom to a marriage, but they must be judged realistically regarding the degree of tension they may cause. This is especially true if you come from different ethnic backgrounds, where traditions and expectations often differ greatly.

What we bring from our families of origin may also affect the degree to which we struggle to "leave" home. You can cleave to your spouse only to the extent that you leave . . . your mother and father, that is. The word "leave" used in Genesis 2:24 speaks very specifically of starting a new primary relationship. Certainly you should have an ongoing and hopefully close and supportive relationship with your parents, but your primary relationship is now with each other. You are not being grafted into the family tree; you are starting a new sapling.

Leaving means you transfer your allegiance to your spouse. If a situation comes up where the desires of your mother and spouse conflict, you are to be more concerned about hurting your spouse than hurting your mother. Leaving means you are no longer responsible for obeying your parents—but still you honor them.

Many couples get a glimpse of this during the planning for their wedding. Are you walking on eggshells because you are afraid your mom will not agree with your desires?

Have your vacations all been with family, and to where mom and dad decide to go? Is the expectation that all vacations and holidays will be spent with family? There is nothing wrong with doing these things, unless you are not free to do what you wish to do with your lives.

Too many children are not free to start their married lives in a healthy manner because they are still trying to stay bonded with their parents and to please them, over and above cleaving to their spouse.

The interesting fact is that it is only after you have truly left mother and father and made your spouse your priority, confidante, and best friend that you will be able to return as an adult to your family without the relationship being a threat or unhealthy alliance.

Making It Personal

- Are you at all embarrassed when your boyfriend or girlfriend is with you in your parents' home or visits your family?

- Does your friend indicate that many differences make it hard to be with your family?

- Is there a sense that your family is better, or that your family is looked down on?

- Do you get a knot in your stomach at the suggestion that both sets of parents get together?

- How do you respond to the thought of the other's parents living with you?

- Do you feel supported by your future in-laws?

Making It Plural

Jot down notes and discuss the areas this question confirmed for you or the issues that were raised in your mind which merit further discussion.

Circle the number that best represents how you feel about your relationship in light of The Family Background Question.

10	9	8	7	6	5	4	3	2	1

Extremely confident   ⟵——————⟶   Extremely hesitant

17 / *The Public and Private Question*

Do you like your date both in public and in private?

Do you like your special friend when you are in public? Are you proud to be there as a couple? Does the other do well when you are out with new people, or do you find yourself having to "lead" whenever you are out?

Jill and Pete did fine when they were alone. She didn't seem to mind his shyness when it was just the two of them. She had never had a boyfriend before she met and later married Pete. She was definitely a people person, and was constantly involved in public events. She had many friends and was the life of the party. He, on the other hand, was a farmer. He loved to work alone and actually did not buy more land because it would have meant that he needed to hire people. He was pleasant, but did not take much initiative, especially when it came to interacting with people. When they went out in public, Jill was almost embarrassed to be with him. He didn't seem to have ever received training in basic social skills. At a meal, he would start eating as soon as he was served, never waiting for the hostess to begin. He would stand around at parties, mindlessly following Jill because he was so uncomfortable by himself. If asked a question, he would respond, but he seldom took the initiative to ask someone about him or herself. He generally looked down and avoided eye contact when he was with people. He was once fired from his job at an ice cream shop when he was in high school simply because he made the customers nervous. In order to cope with her embarrassing husband, Jill began to attend functions by herself. This was fine with Pete, since he didn't like folks much anyway. Before long, Jill became more involved in out-of-the-house activities and Pete became even more isolated.

Some couples seem to be able to adjust to each other and make allowances for one another when they are alone together, but find it more challenging when in public. Because so much of life is in public, be sure you are comfortable with and proud of the other—not embarrassed or ill at ease—when you are in social settings together.

Do you enjoy being together when you are alone in a private setting? Some couples do great as long as they are leading a Bible study, participating in a mission trip, or singing in the praise band together. How about when it's just the two of you and no other people are around and no activities are going on?

Bill was the leader of the Bible study, and soon noticed Sally. He eventually asked her to co-lead the study. It was awesome. She respected how thoroughly he prepared for each study. He was always witty, yet caring, and deep at the same time. Whenever he was up front, she was so proud. Whenever she asked him about going out, Bill always responded with enthusiasm: "That's a great idea; I'll invite some friends to join us." Dinner was a comedy act in itself. Bill was hilarious and the center of attention. As the couples would leave, someone usually commented to Sally, "You sure are lucky to be dating Bill. I bet life is one laugh after another."

Sally told us, "The reality is that life is one laugh after another, as long as we are in public. In private, however, it is a different story. He often is short with me. He seems almost bored to be alone with me. He wants all our activities to be with others. Our nights are filled with going out or having couples over—it seems we are seldom alone."

It is extremely important that we know we have been chosen individually as covenant partners and not simply as part of a public ministry. Much of life will be spent with one's own family. Some people are comfortable only in public because there they never have to reveal who they really are. They are not interested in more intimate environments, such as alone time at home, where issues that are personal or probing might come up. Examine your comfort level both when you are together in public *and* when you are together in private, because this will be your partner 24/7.

Making It Personal

- Are you comfortable with your future mate at a more formal dinner party?

- Does your date interact well with your friends at an event?

- How do your friends feel about your future spouse?

- Go out to dinner with your parents and observe your date's interaction with them.

- Are you able to be alone together and share deeply?

- Is the majority of your time together spent with other friends?

- Does your potential spouse become a significantly different person in public than when the two of you are alone?

- Would you be comfortable riding in a car for 10 hours together without a radio or CD player?

Making It Plural

Jot down notes and discuss the areas this question confirmed for you or the issues that were raised in your mind which merit further discussion.

Circle the number that best represents how you feel about your relationship in light of The Public and Private Question.

10   9   8   7   6   5   4   3   2   1

Extremely confident   ⟵——————⟶   Extremely hesitant

How much do your passions overlap?

Do you each have passions that burn within you—things you want to accomplish during your days on earth? Are your passions similar? I'm not suggesting you both need to have the same call, but are your passions in conflict with each other? Does one of you have a passion for world evangelism and missions, and see your future overseas, while the other has a passion for computers and a nine-to-five job that allows you to stay in the same suburb and go to the same church for the rest of your lives? Both are valid passions, but they are definitely in conflict with each other.

A summer camp staff member who was working with high school students was in tears because she had just broken up with her boyfriend, who was working in another state for the summer. The issue that precipitated the breakup was the boyfriend's annoyance that she had not been calling him more frequently. She explained that class time, games, and hanging out with campers often took her right up to curfew, at which time the phones were off limits. The boyfriend told her that she should cut short her time with the campers so she could call him each night. She explained that while she would like to talk, her responsibilities and her love for the girls with whom she worked kept her from having time to call him except on the weekends. He continued to apply pressure on her to decide what was most important, and she did—by choosing to break up with him.

The girl was passionate about ministry; she came alive in such settings. Her boyfriend was passionate about her, but resented her passion taking her away from him.

Some people have a passion for sports. They "come alive" when they are coaching or playing sports. It would be good for them to marry someone who also has a passion for sports.

It could even be that you both have a passion for ministry, but in different areas. One of you may *love* children—if you could have your way you would hold babies the rest of your life. Your partner might see babies only as a necessary nuisance along the way to the teen years where his passions and interests in child-raising are greatest.

You need to share the same passions. Often the difference between a successful and an unsuccessful person in ministry, for example, is whether both husband and wife share the same passion, even if only one of them is actually employed in the ministry.

> *A large church had a junior high pastor who was recognized as one of the best. He spent time preparing for his classes, going to events at church, and hanging out with kids. Then he married a woman who had a high-pressure Monday-through-Friday job. After the wedding, his effectiveness dropped significantly. She resented the fact that he had to work on the weekends— their only "free time" together. Soon he started cutting back from attending weekend events and the sporting and cultural events in which his kids were participating. Before long, he resigned from the church.*

The same principles apply in vocations outside of Christian ministry. I am not saying you have to have identical passions, but what I am saying is that if you are "passionate" about your passions and your spouse does not share those passions, it will become easy to go your individual ways and not share these areas of life with each other. Too often, in marriage, when individuals go their separate ways to pursue their passions, each may find another who shares that passion as well, and an "unwholesome passion" can easily develop. Author John Eldredge writes, "don't ask yourself what the world needs, ask yourself what makes you come alive, because what the world needs are *men* who have come alive" (*Wild at Heart*, p. 206). But make sure that your "coming alive" does not kill your marriage.

Making It Personal

- Before you started dating, did your friend share your passion?

- Have you seen ways in which he or she is supportive or resentful of your involvement in your passion?

- Does your date have a passion?

- If your passions are different, how do you see them affecting you after marriage?

- What would it take for you to give up your passion?

- What if you were forced to choose between marrying and pursuing your passion?

Making It Plural

Jot down notes and discuss the areas this question confirmed for you or the issues that were raised in your mind which merit further discussion.

Circle the number that best represents how you feel about your relationship in light of The Shared Passion Question.

10	9	8	7	6	5	4	3	2	1

Extremely confident ⟵⟶ Extremely hesitant

19 / The Finance Question

Do you have similar views of finances and stewardship?

How do you handle finances? Do you both have savings accounts? How do you deal with credit cards? Do you carry a balance? What sort of debt are you bringing into marriage? Is your significant other spending money on non-essentials instead of paying off debt? What about tithing? Do you plan to start tithing "when you have more money"? Our experience is that one who does not tithe with a little, will likely not tithe with a lot.

A couple came in for marital advice. They were under enormous stress and did not know whether their marriage would survive. One of their biggest sources of stress was their finances. When asked if there were any "big ticket" items they could eliminate from their spending, they identified three. First, their monthly payments of $500 each for their luxury automobiles; second, the expense of the 2,000-square-foot addition they were putting on their house; and third, the $13,000 they were spending annually on private education for their children. But they were not willing to adjust these. They were not willing to give up their cars, the house had to be finished, and the education of their children was a priority. Because their children were only 3 and 5 years old, it was suggested that the children would likely benefit more from a less stressful home environment than from private schools. Sadly, like the rich young ruler (Luke 18:23), this couple went away sorrowful . . . but unchanged.

Finances are a huge area of tension in many marriages and yet many enter marriage convinced they can live on love and little else. It is extremely important to understand each other's financial habits before you marry, and to make sure you are both committed to financial responsibility. I strongly recommend not going into debt for anything except emergencies. A new bedroom set or new car is not an emergency. What sort of budget have you established for the first years of marriage? How do you plan to handle tithing?

What kind of credit card debt does he/she have? Does the card get paid off each month? If there is a balance, is he spending money on luxuries such as expensive coffee drinks, movie rentals, and restaurant meals rather than paying off the card? How have you seen her habits in the area of "immediate gratification?" Is she willing to do without until the item desired is on sale, or does she need to have it now? Does she see another pair of shoes as a "need" instead of a "want" that does not need to be catered to?

> *A young graduate student receives just $10,000 per year for her services as a full-time graduate assistant. Remarkably, she pays all her bills, tithes, and saves. Her choices on housing, car, and entertainment have all been made in such a way to stay within her budget. It would have been easy for her to insist on better housing, a different car, or more meals out and just "put it on the card" . . . but she doesn't.*

One of the most frequent mistakes made is the assumption that once you earn more money, all monetary issues will be solved. Virginia and I meet regularly with NFL players whose marriages are torn with tension over finances. Make sure you have worked through some material on finances and are on the same page—and make sure the ink on the bottom line is black and not red.

Past performance, while not a guarantee, is still the best indicator of future expectations. Someone who didn't save before marriage will not likely save after. If you were not willing to delay purchasing some particular clothing you "had to have" before you were married, you will likely have difficulty in delaying purchases after marriage.

Making It Personal

- Do you have saving accounts?

- How have you observed delayed gratification in each other when it comes to purchases?

- Do you have any credit card debt? Why? If you do, when do you plan to pay it off?

- Do you have any loans? If so, what's the payment plan?

- What percentage of your gross income are you each tithing each month?

- How many times do you eat out during a normal week?

- If you are in debt, when was the last time you went more in debt on a non-necessary item?

- How important is it to you to have name-brand clothes?

- How have you decided what make, model, and year of car to own?

- For what items do you feel it is acceptable to go into debt?

Making It Plural

Jot down notes and discuss the areas this question confirmed for you or the issues that were raised in your mind which merit further discussion.

Circle the number that best represents how you feel about your relationship in light of The Finance Question.

10   9   8   7   6   5   4   3   2   1

Extremely confident   ⟵————⟶   Extremely hesitant

Questions on
*C*hemistry

What role does physical attraction play in your relationship?

Do you have "chemistry"? If there is no chemistry, you may form a working partnership but lack the spark needed to ignite the explosively passionate marriage that God desires for couples.

> *The young man was talking to his mentor about his relationship with his girlfriend of two years when he shared he had no physical attraction for her. She was the most Godly, hardest-working, fun, energetic, creative woman he knew, but he had no physical attraction for her. The mentor said, "Marry her anyway; the physical will come." The mentee said, "I have not remained a virgin for 25 years merely to hope physical attraction will come."*

The young man was right. Physical and sexual attraction is not the foundation on which to build a house, but without it there is little laughter, joy, or delight in the walls.

Some couples will boast that the physical purity part of their relationship is going well. "We have no problem in this area," they may say. If you have been dating for a while and are contemplating marriage and "have no problem in this area," you have a problem. You should be fighting with all your might to stay pure—there definitely should be a strong sexual desire for each other. As you leave mother and father and move toward a lifelong commitment to each other, it is right and natural to have a desire to "seal the covenant" with sexual intercourse, as theologian Dr. Gordon Hugenberger would say.

One whole book of the Bible is devoted to the delights of the sexual relationship and strong attraction of a husband and wife. In this book, Song of Solomon, the author constantly uses the metaphor of wine to describe the delights of the sexual relationship.

> How delightful is your love, my sister, my bride!
> How much more pleasing is your love than wine, and the
> fragrance of your perfume than any spice!
> —Song of Solomon 4:10

Such an attraction is not only allowed, it is essential to the relationship. Without a romantic, sexual component, you really have a roommate situation—which is not how marriage was designed to be.

The marriage relationship is so strong that couples who are "intoxicated" with love for each other will be "out of their minds" while making love. The sexual relationship is a gift from God to help couples experience a bit of the unity, oneness, delight, and ecstasy there is in the Trinity. Song of Solomon 5:1 shows most clearly God's delight with the marital sexual relationship when He states there:

> "Eat, O friends, and drink; drink your fill, O lovers."

God is glorified by marital sexual union because it fulfills His design for husband and wife.

> I have come into my garden, my sister, my bride; I have gathered
> my myrrh with my spice. I have eaten my honeycomb and my
> honey; I have drunk my wine and my milk.
> Eat, O friends, and drink; drink your fill, O lovers.
> —Song of Solomon 5:1

The use of this sexual relationship outside of marriage is intoxicating as well, but in this case, one's judgment is significantly impaired by his or her intoxication.

With her the kings of the earth committed adultery and the inhabitants of the earth were intoxicated with the wine of her adulteries."   — Revelation 17:2

Is sex the glue that holds a marriage together? No. But sex is a wonderful gift to a husband and wife, and God not only encourages, but *commands* couples to engage in it regularly—*after* they are married.

Making It Personal

- Do you both have a desire to express yourselves more fully to each other physically?

- Is it difficult to not become too involved physically?

- Do you contemplate with expectation and pleasure the day you can become one physically?

Making It Plural

Jot down notes and discuss the areas this question confirmed for you or the issues that were raised in your mind which merit further discussion.

Circle the number that best represents how you feel about your relationship in light of The Physical Attraction Question.

10	9	8	7	6	5	4	3	2	1

Extremely confident ⟵——————⟶ Extremely hesitant

How have you encouraged each other towards sexual purity?

The sexual relationship, designed by God, is so wonderful that God gives clear guidance in scripture so that couples are able to experience all He has for them sexually. The writer of Song of Solomon says three times, "don't awaken love until it is ripe." (The Message) Love is a powerful force and so wonderful that the new bride tells her friends not to express themselves sexually with another until it is time to do so. The time to do so is within the marriage relationship.

Does your significant other follow God's Word rather than hormones? Knowing your mutual commitment to scripture in this area should bring confidence to you as a couple. If you are both Christians and are sexually active with each other before marriage, there is no reason to believe your spouse will be faithful to you after marriage. Ultimately, what will keep couples faithful to each other is a commitment to follow God's Word—regardless of feelings, desires, happiness, or hormones. There is a likelihood that, at some point in your marriage, your spouse will meet someone who is more sensitive, more attractive, more affirming, or more engaging than you. At times like this, you want to have the confidence that comes from knowing that, when the hormones were raging before marriage, you both chose to honor God and each other over your emotions and hormones.

> *A couple came in for counseling. The husband had just been caught in an adulterous affair. His wife was screaming at him, "How could you do this to me? What's wrong with you? I just can't understand how you could have sex with another woman!" After what seemed an appropriate time, the counselors observed, "You should have some idea how this could happen, since you were the woman with whom he had the affair that ended his first marriage."*

Why would she think he would be faithful to her when he had not been faithful to his first wife? What would lead you to believe the other's character would change? Commitment to scripture must overrule emotions, feelings, and hormones.

How are you both making decisions about physical involvement? Far too many couples take their cues from culture rather than from scripture. Scripture is quite clear regarding how one should handle oneself sexually. In the Song of Solomon, three times the daughters of Jerusalem are urged not to awaken or arouse love until its time—until it is ripe. Scripture is clear that the time for sexual intercourse is after marriage (Genesis 2:24). God gives guidelines for sexual involvement not because He is against sex—He created it, after all—but because He wants married couples to enjoy it fully.

Consider the following four scriptures which give guidance on how to conduct one's self in a way that provides the best foundation for sexual fulfillment in marriage:

- No sexual intercourse before marriage. (Matthew 19:5)
- Do not be selfish in your love. (1 Corinthians 13:5)
- Treat each other in all purity. (1 Timothy 5:2)
- Do not lust after each other. (1 Thessalonians 4:3–5)

Put together along with Song of Solomon 2:7, these scriptures teach us that any form of sexual stimulation should be reserved for marriage. This includes fondling, being naked together, mutual masturbation, and oral sex. Sexual stimulation is a gift of God to prepare couples to fully express their oneness sexually with each other. Once aroused it is very difficult to stop short of sexual intercourse both physiologically and psychologically, because our bodies and minds were not designed to stop. That is why outside of marriage we should not start!

There is no area that blinds couples more to their challenges than premature sexual involvement. For many today, sex has become a recreational sport, something fun to do with a companion: they ski, rollerblade, hike, and have sex. But God's design is that sexual intimacy is to be expressed only within the security of the marriage relationship.

Listen to this woman describe her personal conflict as she tries to make decisions regarding her relationship with her boyfriend:

> I am feeling very drained from my relationship with Sam. I'm tired. I give so much and sacrifice so much and feel like I get nothing in return. He lacks initiative and leadership, and I'm so exhausted from trying to be the leader and the planner of everything. I try to find the ways in which he displays his love for me, and I all come up with is our very sinful physical relationship, which we have tried many times to tone down ... I am more convicted than ever that I want our physical relationship to end, so we can really work on our love for each other and how we display affection, trust, and loyalty.

What a sad email. Perhaps the saddest part is that she considers their "sinful physical relationship" as the way "he displays his love for me." If this guy loved her, he would get off his rear end, take initiative in sacrificially serving her, and honor her by keeping his hands off of her and his pants zipped up.

To confuse sexual involvement with "love" is like saying, "We must love each other because we both like sushi." God created sex to be pleasurable and an expression of love, but never the indication of love.

I remember a woman telling me that her boyfriend had drawn

a clear line before kissing and said he would not kiss her unless they had a commitment to marry. She said, "It was so good not to have to question if the reason he wanted to be with me was for what he could 'get' from me. He showed his love for me in many non-sexual ways, such as outings together and romantic cards." As important as sex is in a marriage relationship, you want to be sure your enjoyment of being together is not linked to it. Best friends can become great lovers, but "premature lovers" are less likely to become best friends.

There are many times in marriage that the sexual relationship is not possible for a variety of reasons. You want to make sure you enjoy each other while making the bed together and not just while in it.

Making It Personal

- How have you come to determine your standards for sexual expression prior to marriage?

- Do either of you have any reservations about the way you are expressing yourselves?

- Would you have any problem sharing your level of involvement with your parents, pastor, and spiritual mentor?

- If you are presently letting your hormones drive your decisions, what leads you to believe you will act differently if and when your hormones begin to rage over someone other than your spouse after marriage?

Making It Plural

Jot down notes and discuss the areas this question confirmed for you or the issues that were raised in your mind which merit further discussion.

Circle the number that best represents how you feel about your relationship in light of The Physical Involvement Question.

10	9	8	7	6	5	4	3	2	1

Extremely confident ⟵——————⟶ Extremely hesitant

Conclusion

Bonus / The "Gut" Question

When all is said and done, what does your gut say about this relationship?

Does your gut consistently yell, "Yes! I am going to marry this person and we will be together for the rest of our lives! I am definitely marrying up!" Or do you have doubts? If you do, listen to them. You should be able to walk down the aisle with complete confidence, not simply with hopes or dreams, but with the certainty that this person is the one for you. Too many couples walk down the aisle thinking:

- "(S)he was the best I could find."
- "I believe (s)he will become all I desire."
- "My folks said we were great for each other."
- "I can't imagine being single the rest of my life."

A young bride was shocked to see the way her fiancé flirted with her bridesmaids during the week-long gathering before the wedding. Two nights before the wedding, she challenged her fiancé on some of his very inappropriate sexual remarks to one bridesmaid in particular. Her challenge was met with a string of expletives that shocked the bride-to-be. She walked down the aisle at her wedding disillusioned, but hopeful that what she had seen was a bad dream and not a preview of a marital nightmare. She was wrong.

It is normal to have some jitters before a wedding. This is a big change in life! But if there is a real check in your spirit,

135

don't move ahead. Contracts can be cancelled simply by paying a penalty; covenants are cancelled at enormous cost to all who are involved.

I remember that in my own life one of the "gut" confirmations came when I met other attractive women. Instead of saying to myself "she might be interesting," I found myself thinking, "I sure am glad to be in love with Virginia." Another indicator came one December when I went to my parents' home—two hours away—for my youngest sister Carol's birthday. Normally I would have stayed the weekend, but though I loved my family very much, after the party I excused myself to drive back to San Diego—or more accurately, to Virginia. I was "leaving" mother and father for Virginia.

On the other hand, be careful not to try to "talk" your gut into marriage. If parents, friends, and mentors are voicing their concerns about your upcoming marriage, and you are the only one "hearing God's voice," check your hearing.

Making It Personal

- Have you had a consistent peace about your plans to marry?

- Have any significant people in your life given you any reason to pause?

- Do you look forward to a life together with incredible joy, or do you foresee significant effort to make it work?

- Does the thought of heading off as husband and wife thrill you or scare you?

Making It Plural

Jot down notes and discuss the areas this question confirmed for you or the issues that were raised in your mind which merit further discussion.

Circle the number that best represents how you feel about your relationship in light of The "Gut" Question.

10   9   8   7   6   5   4   3   2   1

Extremely confident   ⟵——————⟶   Extremely hesitant

Are all the categories weighted equally?

All four categories are important; however, in our experience the conviction category should be weighted most heavily. This is the category that ultimately will drive your decisions and actions. If you identify yourself as a Christian but your potential mate does not identify with your faith, scripture clearly states you should not move toward marriage (2 Corinthians 6:14). If you do not share a view of the authority of scripture, then in my opinion, you should not move ahead toward marriage, since your source of absolute authority is not shared.

Character is also extremely important, as it is the expression of your convictions. You may marry someone who is not a servant-hearted person—but the question is, why would you? People without strong character tend to siphon energy rather than infuse it.

Compatibility makes life fun, vital, and much more interesting. Since you are covenanting to live with this person the rest of your life, it makes sense to marry someone with whom you share a majority of interests and passions.

Chemistry is often the initial draw, but is not the cement that holds a relationship together. If physical involvement is developed too quickly, it has the potential of blinding one to the deficiencies of a partner. On the other hand, marriage without chemistry is like a sunrise without color. The marriage may be functional, but it's not the way it was designed to be and not nearly as much fun.

Virginia and I were recently privileged to speak to a marriage-and-family class of 50 at a public university. The topic the professor had asked us to address was "Making wise decisions in choosing a life partner." We asked the class what characteristics they wanted in a life partner and listed their responses on the board in the front of the classroom. One student volunteered "understanding"; then another raised her hand and said, "faithful"; another said, "good provider"; and so the list went on: not selfish, good with children, disciplined, forgiving, fun, similar interests, likes my family, good-looking, and so on.

After one side of the board was full of their desired characteristics in a mate, we made four columns and put the words Convictions, Character, Compatibility, and Chemistry at the tops of the columns. We asked the class which of those they felt played the most significant role in relationships on campus. Unanimously they voiced Chemistry. We asked for what was next in importance, and Compatibility was their choice, followed by Character and then Convictions. We then asked the class to arrange their desirable characteristics of a life partner into the columns in which they felt those characteristics best fell. They were amazed as the words were transferred one-by-one: the vast majority of the items fell under Character and Convictions. In fact, only one fell into the Chemistry column.

No wonder relationships are struggling so. We make our decisions regarding relationships on the very things that are least important for a lasting relationship. Remember that all four of these categories are necessary, but the weight given each and the order they are entered into is critical.

When relationships are built on chemistry, the chemistry must remain high in order to keep the relationship vital. The class recognized quickly that if chemistry and sexual appeal were the glue that held relationships together, then rich and beautiful people would have the most lasting relationships. The problem in putting so much weight on the chemistry component is that it tends to blur our vision of the other three categories. God has designed the sexual relationship to be extremely powerful. Within the marriage relationship, sex is designed to be an expression of oneness, intimacy, passion, and abandonment. Within marriage, it can be that which blocks out all the issues of the day as the couple become enraptured in the moment with each other.

Outside of the marriage relationship, sex is still powerful and can easily feel like true intimacy, but it actually blocks you from seeing the real "issues" of the relationship. That is why I believe the Shulamite wife in Song of Solomon repeats three times to her single lady friends, "Do not arouse or awaken love until it so desires" (Song of Solomon 2:7; 3:5; 8:4). She is essentially saying "this sex thing is so strong; don't get it going until you are in a lifelong covenant relationship."

> *A couple lived together for a year and a half before they were convicted that they should live separately and be sexually abstinent until their marriage some nine months later. The woman said it meant a great deal to her to know that her fiancé loved being with her even when there was no sexual relationship. She confided that in their sexual relationship she would feel pressure to please him sexually in order to "keep" him. He, on the other hand, admitted that he did not mention things that bothered him about her out of fear she would be upset and would not have sex with him that night. Neither of them was truly getting to know each other, because they were relating out of performance and a fear of losing each other.*

There are some couples that remain "technical virgins" yet are so heavily involved physically that their vision regarding each other is significantly blurred. That is why I believe the Shulamite said, "Do not arouse or awaken love . . ."

Some couples consider their compatibility along with chemistry in making this lifelong decision. They have a good physical relationship and they both enjoy rock climbing, tennis, or the theater. What else could be greater, rock climbing by day and sex at night? The problem with this logic is that our bodies deteriorate and our sexual attraction can fade. Because of age and stage, the ability to do those "compatibility" activities may wane.

In actuality, a deficit in character and convictions often affects our enjoyment of the chemistry and compatibility areas of our relationship. If you are angry with your mate because of his self-ishness or her nagging, and you are arguing about your convictions regarding values and absolutes, you likely will not want to do things together, and the only chemistry experienced will be the explosions of mixing two volatile individuals together.

When convictions are given the most weight in a relationship, couples first look at shared values that will drive their life choices. These areas include the faith aspect of their relationship. Do they agree on absolute authority or what it is, if there is one? Are their faiths the same? If both are Christians, do they have a similar passion for faith expression? This also includes their view of scripture. Is it authoritative in the decision-making process regarding lifestyle choices? Shared convictions are foundational to strong agreement in character issues.

Character in many ways is an expression of convictions. Someone once said character is who you are when no one is looking. I would add that character is also who you are when you are not feeling especially warm toward someone you are with. Character is who you really are. Often couples make life-long decisions regarding each other in rather "surreal" situations. Virginia and I recently counseled a couple; in his first marriage the man had felt, and expressed, a lot of rage. When the newly engaged couple was asked about how they deal with conflict, the couple said they had never had an argument. This would be an example of a woman being so taken with the "chemistry and compatibility" that she has not taken stock of his character or his history of anger. He has suppressed it for a while, but you can be sure it will show itself when the "pressure to impress" is over.

Other expressions of character occur in the areas of servant-hood, hospitality, compassion, and leadership. These are the day-to-day expressions of who someone is.

In our experience, couples who share convictions and have strong character often truly have more areas of "compatibility" that span different ages and stages. We also have found that when couples have a deep shared vital faith that expresses itself in strong character, they have a "chemistry" for each other that continues to grows as long as they live.

One of my favorite couples of all time are Claude and Forestine. They met many, many years ago when he was a salesman for a company and she was a secretary (it was okay to call them that back then). Claude was attracted to Forestine's character in the way she did her work and treated others. Forestine was attracted to Claude because of the way he treated those "beneath" him. He was a man of integrity and compassion. They soon found that they both had a passion for their relationship to the Lord. Over the years, Claude and Forestine have been faithful to the Lord and to each other, and have cared for those God brought their way. They have done some great things for the Kingdom, but few will know who they are.

A number of years ago, my wife and I taught an adult Sunday school class; Claude and Forestine attended this class for some years. One fall, we started a three-week series on marital sexuality. I actually didn't expect Claude and Forestine to attend the series—after all, they were already in their 80s—but they attended all three weeks. After the third week, in which we spoke quite frankly about the physical aspects of marital sexuality, Claude came up to me after class and said, "This series on sexuality is the best series you have ever done. There has been so much huggin' and kissin' in our house these last three weeks—streaking, too!" I try not to envision those in our class, but I have a vivid mental picture of Claude and Forestine chasing each other around their house buck naked, and I thought, "they have it!" At 80 years of age, they understand more about sexual intimacy than most couples in their 20s will ever learn. Claude and Forestine were drawn to each other because of their shared convictions and character. They had similar passions and enjoyed compatibility in many areas and, because of all this, experienced a lasting intimacy and chemistry into their old age. I wish this for you.

Now What?

How did you do? How do you feel? What questions were raised? One of three results will likely come out from this experience.

- Confirmation: You have read and contemplated the questions, and feel more than ever you are right for each other. We would suggest going over the list with some folks you know well, whom you respect as Godly mentors, and ask them to read the questions and see if they have any areas of concern for you. Sometimes we have relational "blind spots" because we so badly want a relationship to work. If all continue to affirm your relationship, move ahead prayerfully and joyfully.

- Caution: Perhaps the experience has raised some issues you feel need further exploration. We would suggest you seek counsel in those areas and don't move ahead until you are confident. Dealing with issues before marriage is a lot easier and healthier than waiting until after marriage.

- Cancellation: Perhaps the issues raised have led you to end the relationship. This is often a very painful decision, but a much better one than forcing the relationship, only to deal with these significant issues after marriage.

May God guide you and give you His joy, peace and confirmation as you seek His best for your lives.

About the Author

Dr. Paul Friesen has been married for 33 years to his wife, Virginia, and they are the parents of three young adult girls, the eldest of whom was married in February 2007. Paul and Virginia are the founders of Home Improvement Ministries (www.HIMweb.org), a non-profit organization dedicated to equipping individuals and churches to better encourage marriages and families in living out God's design for healthy relationships.

Paul writes, teaches, and counsels. He and Virginia regularly speak together at marriage, men's, and women's conferences across the country, as well as at family and parenting seminars. The Friesens are (with four others) co-authors of the book *Restoring the Fallen* published by InterVarsity Press. In 2006, Home Improvement Ministries published Paul's book *Letters to My Daughters*, and his book *So You Want to Marry My Daughter?* in 2007. Together with his wife he has also written a daily marriage devotional guide, *In Our Image: Marriage as a Reflection of the Godhead*, published in 2008.

Each summer, the Friesens travel to California to serve as program directors for InterVarsity Christian Fellowship's Campus by the Sea family camp programs.

Paul has a doctorate in Marriage and Family Therapy and a master's degree in Family Ministry, both from Gordon-Conwell Theological Seminary. Before founding Home Improvement Ministries in 2003, he was on staff at Grace Chapel in Lexington, Massachusetts, where he served as the Director of Men's and Family Ministries.

Paul and Virginia's greatest joy in life is knowing that their children are "walking in the truth."

Other books and study guides
authored or co-authored by Paul or Virginia Friesen
and available from Home Improvement Ministries:

Restoring the Fallen, InterVarsity Press

Letters to My Daughters, Home Improvement Ministries

So You Want to Marry My Daughter?, Home Improvement Ministries

Recapturing Eden, Home Improvement Ministries

Engagement Matters, Home Improvement Ministries

In Our Image, Home Improvement Ministries

Raising a Trailblazer, Home Improvement Ministries

~

For more information about Home Improvement Ministries, or to book
Paul and Virginia Friesen for a speaking engagement, or to order any of our
products, please write, e-mail, fax, or call us:

Call: 781-275-6473

Fax: 781-275-6469

E-mail: info@himweb.org

Write: Home Improvement Ministries
         209 Burlington Road, Suite 105
         Bedford, MA 01730 USA

Online: www.HIMweb.org/books   (for the online bookstore)
         www.HIMweb.org/speak   (to book the Friesens for speaking)
         www.HIMweb.org/fb   (to reach us on Facebook)